THE

Joshua

GENERATION

THE Joshua GENERATION

Restoring the
Heritage of
Christian Leadership

MICHAEL FARRIS

BROADMAN
&HOLMAN
PUBLISHERS
NASHVILLE, TENNESSEE

10-Digit ISBN: 0805426086
13-Digit ISBN: 9780805426083

Published by Broadman & Holman Publishers,
Nashville, Tennessee

Dewey Decimal Classification: 306.43
Subject Heading: EDUCATIONAL SOCIOLOGY \
HOME SCHOOL

Unless otherwise noted, Scripture quotations are from
the Holy Bible, New International Version, copyright ©
1973, 1978, 1984 by International Bible Society. Other version used is nasb, the New American Standard Bible, ©
the Lockman Foundation, 1960, 1962, 1963, 1968, 1971,
1972, 1973, 1975, 1977, 1995; used by permission.

1 2 3 4 5 6 7 8 9 10 09 08 07 06 05

Dedication

This book is dedicated to the thousands of Christian young people who have the potential to lead our nation and shape our culture.

I would like to express my deepest gratitude to one of these young people, Naomi Harralson. Naomi, a senior at Patrick Henry College, did substantial research and assisted in all phases of the preparation of this book. She demonstrates what is possible in a young life that is committed to God and the pursuit of excellence.

Table of Contents

Preface

It was Thanksgiving break of 1969. I traveled the 50 miles from Whitman College in Walla Walla, Washington to my home in Kennewick. Whitman is a secular college with a reputation for high academic achievement.

In the course of that weekend, I got into a serious discussion with my father—I have vague memories of there being flashes of anger on both sides. There is no doubt that there was a clash of values.

My father had prayed with me as I accepted Jesus as my personal Savior 12 years earlier on November 9, 1957, when I was six. Our family had faithfully attended First Baptist Church in Kennewick since I was three. I had been very involved in the high school youth group, and my head knowledge of Christianity was excellent.

Even though I only vaguely remember some components of this Thanksgiving conversation, there was one bold statement that I remember with absolute clarity.

"I believe that Christian humanism is the right philosophy of life," I declared.

Something inside of me told me that I had to keep some vestige of Christianity in my worldview. But, look at my wording in the way we are taught to diagram a sentence. The basic sentence is "I believe that humanism is the right philosophy of life." "Christian" was an adjective that only served to modify the noun, "humanism." My own words declared humanism as my core philosophy.

I cannot remember any of my professors at Whitman even using the word "humanism." I can't remember whether I read it in some assigned text. It is even possible that the idea had been implanted in my public high school experience and simply had grown during my time at Whitman.

But I had been converted—at some level at least—away from biblical Christianity into the man-centered religion of humanism. To be a little less hard on myself, it would be most fair to simply call me confused. Indeed, I was mixed up both philosophically and politically.

A year and a half later, I was back to my roots and growing. My personal walk with God was reactivated and alive. My new bride, Vickie, and I were involved in the Navigators. And because of a professor of constitutional law at a new college, Western Washington State College, I was no longer confused politically. Dr. Dick S. Payne taught me the original intent of the Constitution, and I took off like a rocket.

My college experience illustrates the problem. When bright Christian kids are given a secular education, there is a price to be paid. By God's grace I recovered. But not all do. As I explain in this book, the majority of young people who attend church every week when they are 18, no longer are in church when they are 29.

It is high time that Christians look at secular higher education and ask ourselves: *Do we really want the best and the brightest born-again young people educated in the philosophy that dominates American academia?*

Do we want our best to become "Christian humanists" or Christian leaders?

CHAPTER 1

The Joshua Generation: Developing a Vision for True Success

I just love the way that many moms and dads introduce me to their children. I have met countless future senators, governors, presidents, and Supreme Court justices. The parents' glowing descriptions of their children's aspirations while the children stand by with beaming faces give me hope for the future of America.

Most parents are quick to believe that their children will develop into adults with significant life impact. My mother was no exception. It was from her that I learned to believe that nothing is impossible with a God who delights in using those who are faithful to His call.

Even if dreams of generational greatness have dimmed in other quarters, they burn brightly in thousands of home-schooling families. These moms and dads truly believe that their children are called to be the leaders of the future. Their belief is far more specific than the tautology that eventually today's generation of children will replace today's generation of adults. They believe that their own children, in many cases, have unusually high prospects for being the particu-lar people who will rise to the top levels of government, law, journalism, media, religion, art, business, and science. I think they are absolutely right.

While it is difficult to measure the exact number of homeschool students, somewhere between 3 and 5 percent of the school-aged population are being taught by their parents at home. But I am convinced that this small percentage of students will grow into a large percentage of the highest leaders of the next generation who take seriously the Christian assignment of redeeming culture, especially in the most visible vocations, which are the focus of this book. The evidence that leads me to this conclusion falls into three categories.

Academics. First, there is strong evidence of the academic success of homeschooling. Dozens of studies demonstrate that, on average, homeschooled students are far ahead in academic achievement compared to those who attend other schools. The average homeschooled student is approximately at the same achievement level as public school honor students. Another way of saying this is that 50 percent of homeschooled students rank in the top 15 percent of comparable students in the general population.[1] However, academic excellence is only one ingredient for future success; the future belongs not just to the bright, but also to those who engage in the affairs of life.

Activism. Young adults who have been homeschooled are far more likely to be active in the civic affairs of our nation than their age mates from other forms of education. A recent study by the National Home Education Research Institute compared homeschool graduates (ages eighteen to twenty-four) with the general public (eighteen to twenty-four) in the following categories:

- Contributed to a candidate, political party, or political cause:

    Homeschool Grads: 10 percent

    General Public: 1 percent

- Participated in a protest or boycott:

    Homechool Grads: 14 percent

    General Public: 7 percent

- Worked for a candidate, political party, or political cause:

    Homeschool Grads: 14 percent

    General Public: 1 percent

- Voted in national/state election in past five years:

    Homeschool Grads: 76 percent

    General Public: 29 percent

Consider one more comparison: homeschool grads aged eighteen to twenty-four versus the general public aged forty to fifty-four. Again, 76 percent of the homeschooled young people voted in the last five years. Among forty to fifty-four year olds in the general public, only 53 percent voted. Young homeschool grads show more civic responsibility in voting than is typically found in middle-aged adults. That is an incredible comparison showing both the activism and the social maturity of homeschooling grads. However, one can be bright and diligent but lack the spiritual character that as Christians we know is essential for true success.

Spiritual Character. Formal studies can never claim definitively to assess spiritual character. However, anyone who has spent time with a reasonable number of Christian homeschooled teens realizes—and again this is on average—that there is a disproportionately high level of Christian character and spiritual maturity. I see this in my own grown children and in the dozens of homeschooled young adults that I know well. There is no doubt that their spiritual walk has remained consistently ahead of the rank-and-file evangelical kids that I knew growing up in a good, solid, Bible-teaching church. That includes my own walk with God in my late teens since I was basically the same as most of the kids in my church.

While Christian maturity may be hard to measure with a study, it is possible to measure those who drop out of church. The Southern Baptist Convention recently voted on a proposed resolution that would have encouraged all SBC churches to encourage their member families to provide a Christian education for their children in lieu of public schooling. Why would a major denomination even consider such an idea? Tom Elliff, chairman of the Southern Baptist Convention's Council on Family Life, had previously announced the results of a study which found that 88 percent of evangelical children leave church at eighteen never to return again.[2] While this conclusion may seem alarming and may require further analysis, another study by The Barna Group provides confirmation. Barna's research found a significant drop in church attendance among young people in their twenties. It disclosed that among teens who attended church every week, there was a 42-percent drop in the number that attend church every week from age eighteen to age twenty-five and a 58-percent decline from age eighteen to age twenty-nine.[3] Thus, taking only Barna's research into account, for every one hundred teens who attend church regularly, only forty-two will remain in church when they reach age twenty-nine.

One has to wonder whether attending church has much effect on teens who do attend. Barna's research found some alarming trends among born-again teens. Teens were asked: "Think about the choices you face every day. People make their decisions in different ways. When you are faced with a moral or ethical choice, which ONE of the following best describes how you, yourself, decide what to do?" The following responses were given by born-again teens compared to teens in general.

Whatever will make the most people happy or create the least conflict:

> All teens   10 percent
>
> Born-again teens 12 percent

Whatever you think your family or friends would expect you to do:

> All teens   10 percent
>
> Born-again teens   6 percent

Follow a set of specific principles or standards you believe in, that serve as guidelines for your behavior: the Bible

> All teens   7 percent
>
> Born-again teens 12 percent

Follow a set of specific principles or standards you believe in, that serve as guidelines for your behavior: values taught by your parents

> All teens   10 percent
>
> Born-again teens 10 percent

Follow a set of specific principles or standards you believe in, that serve as guidelines for your behavior: other religious input

> All teens   2 percent
>
> Born-again teens   2 percent

Follow a set of specific principles or standards you believe in, that serve as guidelines for your behavior: lessons from past experience

> All teens   1 percent
>
> Born-again teens   1 percent

What you believe most other people would do in that situation

> All teens   3 percent
>
> Born-again teens   2 percent

Whatever feels right or comfortable in that situation

> All teens   38 percent
>
> Born-again teens   34 percent

Whatever will produce the most positive outcome for you, personally

> All teens   16 percent
>
> Born-again teens   13 percent[4]

In another question in the same survey, teens were asked:

> Some people believe that there are moral truths that are absolute, meaning that those moral truths or principles do not change according to the circumstances. Other people believe that moral truth always depends upon the situation, meaning that their moral and ethical decisions depend upon the circumstances. How about you? Do you believe that there are moral absolutes that are unchanging, or that moral truth is relative to the circumstances, or is this something you have never really thought about?

Here are the results:

Moral truth is unchanging

> All teens   6 percent
>
> Born-again teens   9 percent

Depends on the situation

> All teens   83 percent
>
> Born-again teens   76 percent

Don't know

> All teens   11 percent
>
> Born-again teens   15 percent

This means that 47 percent of born-again teens would make moral decisions based on personal positive outcomes or "whatever feels right" versus 12 percent that would follow the Bible and 10 percent that would follow the values taught by their parents. Only 9 percent of born-again teens believe that moral truth is unchanging while 76 percent believe it depends on the situation. It is remarkable how close the born-again teens score compared to teens in general.

We have to ask ourselves: "Why do born again teenagers think so much like teens in general? What ideological sources do they have in common, and what sources are different?" One of the two logical differences would seem to be that born-again teens are more likely than teens in general to attend a church that taught that a person should be born again. The other is that born-again teens are more likely than other teens to have parents who also are born again. (Both of these are educated assumptions on my part.)

The common ideological sources shared by born-again teens with teens in general are public education and the media. The numbers reveal which are more powerful: born-again parents and born-again churches versus public schools and entertainment sources. Most born-again teens have the same values as our secular culture, not the values of their parents and churches.

Look at one other issue and a different survey done by The Polling Company from Washington, D.C. The issue is same-sex marriage. The comparison is between young adults (eighteen to twenty-four) and the age group of their parents (forty-five to sixty-four). Among the parents' generation, 74 percent "strongly agree" that marriage in the United States should exist only between one man and one woman. Among the young adults, only 47.5 percent strongly agree that marriage should be between one man and one woman. An incredible shift in values has occurred in just one generation. What are the sources of this shift in values? Again, the ideological voices that believe that homosexuality is morally equivalent with married heterosexuality come from public education and the media.

To my knowledge, no studies have analyzed whether homeschooled young adults drop out of church or have differing moral convictions from their parents. However, one way to analyze the question is to consider whether homeschooled young people are turning their backs on homeschooling itself, which deeply reflects the values taught by their parents. The 2003 NHERI study found that 95.2 percent of young adults who had been homeschooled were glad that they had been homeschooled; 92.4 percent believed that homeschooling was an advantage to them as an adult. And 82 percent would homeschool their own children. Thus, we can see that 58 percent of regular church-attenders reject the values of their parents (proven by the fact that they stop attending church), whereas at least 82 percent of homeschoolers embrace the values that were core to their families (proven by their desire to homeschool their own children).

Above and beyond all of these statistics, I have the advantage of regularly seeing approximately two hundred homeschooled grads at Patrick Henry College. Excellence in academics, activism, and character has blossomed in nearly all of these young men and women.

I will be the first to recognize that it is not just homeschoolers who will be excellent. I also understand that not all homeschoolers (and not even all born-again homeschoolers) will be morally and academically excellent. In fact, some of my favorite (and most successful) students at

PHC have been students who exclusively attended public schools. (And I truly hope that public and private school students and their parents are reading this book.) The plain fact, however, is that homeschooling is disproportionately producing excellence in all of these categories.

Taking the Land

Many of the discussions I have heard among parents about the success of homeschooling reflect what I call "Moses Generation" kind of thinking. We are so glad that our children are doing well academically compared to the average public school student that we go on endlessly about the educational disparity. There is great satisfaction in seeing our children, again on average, demonstrating far higher levels of moral and spiritual integrity than are found even among Christian children who attend public schools. This also causes us to talk and think like the Moses Generation.

The Moses Generation celebrates the fact that it left Egypt. We like to demonstrate that our educational "manna" is better than the public schools' leeks and onions and melons. And there is no doubt that the Moses Generation of homeschoolers has accomplished something incredibly important. We have broken the notion that education is principally a function of the government. We have taken seriously the requirements of Scripture that command parents to teach their children to love God and know His ways as we go through the ordinary moments of the day.

Yes, leaving Egypt was a big accomplishment, but it is not the end goal. Homeschoolers need to develop a longer view for judging our success. This is true both individually and as a movement.

On an individual level we need to understand that the academic preparation of our children is a means to an end, not the end itself. For example, my daughter Jayme got a perfect score on her annual achievement test in the second grade. I don't mean merely that she scored in the ninety-ninth percentile across the board. She got a perfect score. She gave a correct answer to every single question on the test. Big deal. Jayme is now twenty-seven years old and has two children. If my wife and I judge our success as home-schooling parents by Jayme's second-grade exam, or her SAT scores, or the fact that she graduated from high school at fifteen, we measure our achievement inappropriately. All of these things were encouragements along the way, but they were not the goal. The goal was to raise Jayme with great abilities and a heart that loves God, putting those abilities to use for His kingdom. (Jayme has more than succeeded in this regard as have our other grown children. Among other things she started an organization that is the principal support for a wonderful Christian orphanage in Romania.)[5]

The homeschooling movement needs to develop this same kind of long-range measurement of success that goes far beyond analysis of test scores and victories in spelling bees. On the political front, we should not be content that we have gained recognition of our constitutional right to teach our own children. While these battles are important and will always continue to some degree, homeschool freedom is not the end goal. It is a means to a far greater end.

So what is the standard by which we should judge our long-range success? There is a passage in Hebrews 11 that I would suggest for this purpose:

> And what more shall I say? I do not have time
> to tell about Gideon, Barak, Samson, Jephthah,

David, Samuel and the prophets, who through faith
conquered kingdoms, administered justice, and
gained what was promised; who shut the mouths of
lions, quenched the fury of the flames, and escaped
the edge of the sword; whose weakness was turned
to strength; and who became powerful in battle and
routed foreign armies. (Heb. 11:32–34)

If the Christian homeschooling movement is to call
itself a long-range success, then it must produce a generation of great faith. While the personal faith of each person
and family is the key, we should see works that illustrate
and validate the vibrancy of that faith. James announces
this principle directly. "Show me your faith without deeds,
and I will show you my faith by what I do" (James 2:18). The
passage from Hebrews 11 demonstrates this truth by example. These heroes of faith did great things for God.

How should we judge our success? Do we see our children
administering justice, gaining what was promised, shutting
the mouths of the lions, and quenching the fury of the
flames? Is our weakness turned to strength? Have they become powerful in battle? Have they routed foreign armies?

We should also remember that the battle is not easy. The
remaining verses in Hebrews 11 describe how some heroes
of the faith were jeered at, chained, tortured, stoned, put
in prison, and put to death by the sword. Their failures in
earthly terms were monumental victories in God's terms
because they refused to succumb to fear in light of the heav-
enly promises that awaited them. But this was no excuse not
to fight.

In short, the homeschooling movement will succeed
when our children, the Joshua Generation, engage whole-
heartedly in the battle to take the land.

Take the land. Easy to say. Hard to imagine.

This is the land of MTV, Internet porn, abortion, homosexuality, greed, and accomplished selfishness. This is the land that has forgotten its constitutional principles, and it rules by judicial tyranny and unconstitutional expansion of the power of bureaucracies and agencies that the founding fathers never intended. This is the land that practices socialism while celebrating freedom on the Fourth of July and doesn't even realize the irony.

Yes, there are giants in the land. The task is indeed daunting. But just like the Moses Generation that received the report of the spies, we have to decide whom we are going to believe. Will we look at difficulties and believe in the power of the world? Or will we look at the potential of our children and believe in the power of God?

The goal is not a political coup or the establishment of a New Israel. Although taking the land may certainly include political activism, I am talking about something bigger and broader and longer-lasting. It is a statement about generational greatness that has implications for eternity. It is about raising men and women of faith who, because they love God, refuse to sit silently by while their nation hates what He loves and loves what He hates.

I visited the Soviet Union in 1988. Along with Congressman Frank Wolf and a handful of others, I was there to visit, encourage, and assist Christians and Jews who were suffering from the persecution of the Communist regime. While most groups of Christians we met had families of one or two children like the general population, the Soviet Pentecostals had huge families of six, eight, ten, or more. I asked them why they had such large families. They told me that the rest of their nation was so disheartened with life itself that they did not want to bring too many children into their difficult world. But the Pentecostals viewed it differently. They wanted to say to the world around them, "With Christ life is wonderful, and we prove it to you, even in the midst of our special difficulties, through our children. We bring them into a world with promise." They, of course, were right. And the Iron Curtain fell despite the seeming impossibility of toppling the giants in that land.

I think it is no accident that the homeschooling movement also has so many large families. It is a statement of hope. It is a claim upon the power of God to move our nation through our children.

This book is going to focus on a few of the bigger giants in our land—giants that live in the fields of law, government, journalism, and history. And we are going to look in depth at the elite colleges and universities of our nation. The enemies of freedom and truth dominate these institutions and thereby dominate our nation.

I make no claim to the gift of prophecy. But shortly after I started the Home School Legal Defense Association in 1983, a sense settled in my spirit that our purpose was to win just enough freedom to allow parents to teach their children in the principles of righteousness and freedom that is our spiritual and national heritage. I have long believed that my generation was taking only the first step. The next step would be far bigger. The next generation could, like the generation of the Founding Fathers, have a profound impact for good.

As a result of this belief and confidence in God's plan for the future, I take seriously being introduced to future senators, governors, presidents, and Supreme Court justices. Like their parents, I see great things for our nation through the Joshua Generation.

CHAPTER 2

The Ivy Connection: Elite Education and Leadership

Christians are taught to evaluate leaders principally by looking at spiritual character qualities. We are told that elders should possess a certain set of qualities that would make them men above reproach (1 Tim. 3:1–7). The world at large, however, pays far more attention to other attributes to determine who should be elevated into leadership. In particular, elite academic education is one of the key factors in determining who becomes a leader in modern America—especially in the areas of politics and law.

A recent decision by the Supreme Court highlighted the incredibly high correlation between elite academic education and attainment of the highest levels of leadership in law and politics. In a 2003 majority decision, Justice Sandra Day O'Connor wrote:

> Moreover, universities, and in particular, law schools, represent the training ground for a large number of our Nation's leaders. Individuals with law degrees occupy roughly half the state governorships, more than half the seats in the United States Senate, and more than a third of the seats in the

United States House of Representatives. The pattern is even more striking when it comes to highly selective law schools. A handful of these schools accounts for 25 of the 100 United States Senators, 74 United States Courts of Appeals judges, and nearly 200 of the more than 600 United States District Court judges.[1]

Justice O'Connor neglected to mention that all nine Supreme Court justices attended these elite law schools. She also only noted the effect of attending an elite law school. Other forms of elite academic education produce leaders at the highest level too. For example, President Bush received his undergraduate degree from Yale and his MBA from Harvard. Senate Majority Leader Bill Frist attended Princeton as an undergraduate before going on to Harvard Medical School.

Justice O'Connor proceeded to describe elite education as a process that "cultivate[s] a set of leaders with legitimacy in the eyes of the citizenry."

How does one enter this form of elite education? The first step is high school. Those who have done well in high school have the opportunity to join the ranks of the academic elite in undergraduate school. Those who do well as undergraduates are able to go on to the elite schools of law, medicine, business, and so on. It is rare for students to get into the elite graduate schools unless they were great students back in high school.

What does this have to do with homeschooling? About 15 percent of the public school students would be classified as highly successful as measured by achievement test scores. About 50 percent of the homeschool students reach this same level. Thus, a far greater percentage of homeschool students have the academic potential to enter the path of leadership that is generally considered to "cultivate leaders with legitimacy in the eyes of the citizenry."

Elite education may receive the approbation of the general public, but does it produce a result that is acceptable to serious Christians and consistent with the values of our nation's founding?

Let's think through the impact of college on some of the statistics we considered in the last chapter. The Barna Group's research showed that far more teens attend church than young adults in their twenties. What happened? About 60 percent of the population went to college. Some secularists argue that the mere fact that people become educated has the tendency to reduce reliance on religious faith. My own opinion is that it depends on the dominant philosophical view presented in colleges.

How would one settle the debate between secularists and conservative Christians like me? Does merely being educated produce a greater tendency toward left-wing thinking? Or is it the philosophy of the education that determines the results?

There are no studies on this point that I am aware of, but there is a mountain of experiential evidence. The radical left dominates the campuses of this country. I would posit that the more elite the institution, the more likely it is that the left has achieved nearly total control of the ideological machinery of the institution. (I don't ask you to accept this as a proven conclusion at this point. This is just my thesis. I believe that the evidence is overwhelming for this conclusion, but read the later chapters and decide for yourself.)

What happens when born-again students enter such centers of training? It is common for Christians to look at this situation through rose-colored glasses. We think it is a good idea for Christian students to be sent into secular institutions to do intellectual battles with secularist professors and act as good witnesses to their fellow students. While some students will do this, is this typical? Should we blindly believe that most Christian young people will be stalwarts of the faith in such a setting?

Christian parents and leaders need to wake up to reality. Remember the findings of The Barna Group's research? Among born-again Christian teens, only 22 percent said that the Bible or the values taught by their parents served as the basis of their moral decision-making. The vast majority gave responses that make such teenagers easy targets for left-wing professors: 34 percent base their decisions on whatever feels right or comfortable; 13 percent find the answer that gives the most positive outcome for them personally; 12 percent say they decide moral questions based on what will make most people happy or create the least conflict; 6 percent do what their family or friends expect; and 2 percent would do what most other people would do. This adds up to a total of 67 percent of born-again teens who embrace moral decision-making in some manner that is not likely to help them stand strong in the face of the moral and political onslaught they will receive at college. Moreover, only 9 percent of born-again teens say that moral truth is unchanging, and 76 percent say that it depends on the situation. Mere professions of faith are not going to help when a young person's foundation for decision-making has been so thoroughly eroded before he or she ever sets foot into the college classroom.

Since only 9 percent of born again Christian teens believe that moral truths are absolute, no Christian leader or parent should ever think that most Christian students will stand strong in college. Something has happened to undermine them while they were still in high school. If the high school years have seen this much erosion in their thinking about right and wrong, what would lead anyone to believe that it is going to get better during college? After all, while in high school, students see their parents almost every day and have much closer supervision. Moreover, left-wing teachers are a little more subtle about eroding community values in most high schools. In college, parental supervision of daily living is normally absent and leftist professors could not care less if they offend the traditions of the community— in fact, they would take pride in giving such offenses.

We have seen the hard evidence to demonstrate that church attendance drops off dramatically from age eighteen to age twenty-nine. We need to wake up and see what is obvious. College education which systematically denigrates Christian values is a key factor in this social trend.

Should Christians attend and support colleges that reject and undermine Christian principles?

The Bible is not silent on this subject. The last part of Romans 1 details the consequences of failing to retain the knowledge of God. Note that Romans 1 does not start with those who are openly opposed to Christianity. It describes those who do not think it is worthwhile to retain the knowledge of God.

Most of the elite schools we will discuss in this book were once solid Christian colleges. They may want to pretend that they are not the bitter enemy of Christianity that later chapters in this book will demonstrate. Yet there is not a single secular college that would disagree with the idea that they are no longer basing their educational philosophy on attaining the knowledge of God.

Here is what the apostle Paul says:

Furthermore, since they did not think it worthwhile to retain the knowledge of God, he gave them over to a depraved mind, to do what ought not to be done. They have become filled with every kind of wickedness, evil, greed and depravity. They are full of envy, murder, strife, deceit and malice. They are gossips, slanderers, God-haters, insolent, arrogant and boastful; they invent ways of doing evil; they disobey their parents; they are senseless, faithless, heartless, ruthless. Although they know God's righteous decree that those who do such things deserve death, they not only continue to do these very things but also approve of those who practice them. (Rom. 1:28–32)

Proverbs 13:20 tells us what happens to people who become the companions of fools—that is, those who reject the fear of the Lord as the beginning of knowledge and wisdom: "He who walks with the wise grows wise, but a companion of fools suffers harm."

Some Christians read those passages and say, "That's good enough for me. I understand the danger of sending my son or daughter into an elite college controlled by those the Bible calls fools." But it strikes many other people as a little bit too broad a generalization. Something inside says, "It's not fair to presume that all college professors are left-wing. Sure, there are a few radicals and maybe most are a little more liberal than I, but they will be fair-minded and allow all sides to be presented."

If you think that, you simply do not know what is going on in American higher education. Even though I am the president of a Christian college and a graduate of a secular college and law school,[2] I was astonished when I began to look closely at what was going on in the top colleges and universities in the areas of law, government/political science, history, and journalism. There is no way I can summarize how far removed such schools are from traditional values. You simply have to take a look at the evidence yourself, and that is exactly what we are going to do.

There are at least three good reasons Christians need to look closely at such institutions. First, there is the question of whether a student should attend such an institution. General reliance on a college's reputation, a quick campus visit, or review of a Web site is insufficient. One must discover the general philosophy of the professors at the college—not only in the major the student intends to pursue but also in the core curriculum for general liberal arts requirements.

A second reason concerns financial support. Why would a Christian give money simply because of being an alumnus, liking the football team, or living in the area? Since Christians are only stewards of their money and responsible to God for its use, shouldn't the worldview of the college matter to us before we invest?

Finally, and most importantly for the purposes of this book, if we are going to take back the land, we need to know our philosophical enemies. Even Joshua, who never wavered in his courage, sent a second set of spies to assess the battles they would face.

Elite academic education is the proven path toward leadership in most spheres of cultural influence. But where is it leading us? And should Christians follow this path?

You already know that I believe that this path is dangerous for both Christians and our nation. Let's look at the proof.

CHAPTER 3

The Giants in the Land: The Academic Elite

Homeschoolers and other academically talented Christians face a dilemma upon the completion of their high school education. Do they go to Christian colleges that oftentimes are considered second-rate from an academic perspective? Or do they enter the secular elite colleges and universities that Sandra Day O'Connor described as the recognized "pathways to power" in our society?

Any students considering any college ought to make decisions about their path based on a realistic look at the instruction they will be receiving. It is not enough to see how many faculty members have a Ph.D. or to discover the average class size. No factor in choosing a college is more important than the worldview of the faculty.

No college in America just teaches facts. Nearly every discipline is led by professors holding a Ph.D., which is the abbreviation for "doctor of philosophy." College is far more about philosophy and worldview than it is about the transmission of factoids. And that is the way it should be. However, unlike facts, philosophy is never neutral.

Philosophy takes sides and promotes a larger agenda that we often call a "worldview."

Accordingly, if we want to assess the appropriateness of elite academic education, we need to look past the glitz of their laboratories and massive buildings to understand the philosophies that control these colleges and universities.

Like most people who have been out of college for twenty or thirty years, I thought I had a pretty good idea of what was going on in elite academic circles. I knew that colleges and universities were left of center. That should be no surprise; they were left of center when I was in college in the late 1960s and early 1970s.

However, in preparation for this book, I began to look closely at the actual situation on America's elite campuses. I was astonished at what I found. Liberal Democrats are the conservatives on most college campuses. The dominant philosophy of the American academic community is so extreme that the term "radically left" is but a pale description.

These themes and viewpoints dominate the worldview of elite colleges:

- Diversity is the god of modern education. However, the brand of diversity that is worshipped embraces all lifestyles, all philosophies—provided that those lifestyles and philosophies hold conservatives (and especially conservative Christianity) in disdain. Without shame conservatives on American campuses are pronounced intellectually inferior, ill qualified, and irreversibly backward bigots. While liberal Democrats are ubiquitous, antiwar Green Party members usually outnumber rank-and-file Republicans among faculty members.

- The knowledge of God and a belief in His gift of an unchanging code of moral ethics are ridiculed as belonging only to the unenlightened. "We the people" (which is defined as we the academic elite) is the standard and reality that creates our world.
- Homosexuality and other perverse forms of sexual behavior are not only considered acceptable but also pronounced good and celebrated. Every elite academic campus boasts several prominent openly homosexual professors. Professors teach the goodness of homosexuality, classes are devoted to it, books are written about it, and, predictably, students believe it.
- "Progressive" social programs are the brand of profamily policy advocated on our top campuses. This does not mean that mom and dad should have freedom and responsibility to raise their own children. Rather, "progressivism" means inviting the government to levy taxes in order to provide free universal health and day care and paid family leave.
- Economic socialism is dominant, while outright Marxism holds a respectable minority position.
- America was and is the world's number one terrorist state. Criticism of our nation's history and an attitude of dissent toward those in power are *de rigueur* while any show of patriotism is the ultimate *faux pas*. *Why the Left Hates America* by Daniel Flynn captures the general academic viewpoint. This book focuses almost exclusively on the Left's dominance on college campuses and an unbelievable level of anti-Americanism. Unbelievably, many colleges banned the flying of the American flag after September 11 because it was insensitive to foreign students.

Most Americans will have a hard time understanding how extreme the situation is simply by reading such a summary description. A closer examination is required to comprehend the danger of these giants who have come to occupy our land.

There is no better place to start such a factual inquiry than by looking at the author of one of the most popular college texts on American history. After all, one's views about America today as well as America's future will be profoundly influenced by one's understanding of our past.

America According to Howard Zinn

What would your vision for America's future look like if you believed that the Founding Fathers were greedy, class-oriented villains who masqueraded under a guise of patriotism? If Patrick Henry, Sam Adams, and George Washington did not really believe in liberty, but concocted the War for Independence just to keep the poor under their thumbs, how would this affect your belief in the country they created?

Welcome to the America of Dr. Howard Zinn. In his version of our nation's history—which reads like a Marxist primer—George Washington, James Madison, and their compatriots were not noble souls who risked their lives, fortunes, and sacred honor to build a new nation conceived in liberty but were nothing more than capitalist oppressors who were tired of letting the British have all the power and privilege and merely wanted such trappings for themselves.

Here is how Zinn's best-selling book and acclaimed college text, *A People's History of the United States,* describes America's founding:

> Around 1776, certain important people in the
> English colonies made a discovery that would prove

26

enormously useful for the next two hundred years.
They found that by creating a nation, a symbol, a
legal unity called the United States, they could take
over the land, profits, and political power from
favorites of the British Empire. In the process, they
could hold back a number of potential rebellions
and create a consensus of popular support for the
rule of a new, privileged leadership.[1]

As this passage reveals, Zinn specializes in portraying
past events from the perspective of class conflict. We later
learn that colonial leaders had to win over the vast majority
of colonists to the Revolutionary cause by appealing to their
manufacturing interests and that "the biggest problem was
to keep the propertyless people, who were unemployed and
hungry . . . under control."[2] Farmers-turned-Minutemen
and Indians in Boston harbor were apparently either de-
ceived or coerced. The common colonist who found hope in
grand claims of freedom from tyranny was merely forging
his own chains. Zinn writes:

Those upper classes, to rule, needed to make con-
cessions to the middle class, without damage to their
own wealth or power, at the expense of slaves,
Indians, and poor whites. This brought loyalty. And to
bind that loyalty with something more powerful even
than material advantage, the ruling group found, in
the 1760s and 1770s, a wonderfully useful device.
That device was the language of liberty and equality.[3]

As with the Declaration of Independence, Zinn frames
the Constitution as a pretext for sinister ends. Its guaran-
tees of freedom were a ploy to gain a base of support from
the middle class. These unwitting, working individuals "enable[d] the elite to keep control with a minimum of coercion,

a maximum of law—all made palatable by the fanfare of patriotism and unity."[4] He continues, "What was not made clear [at the adoption of the Constitution]—it was a time when the language of freedom was new and its reality untested—was the shakiness of anyone's liberty when entrusted to a government of the rich and powerful."[5] He portrays the Bill of Rights as little more than a sham.

All six hundred pages of Zinn's volume are permeated with these leftist, ideologically driven sentiments. The problem with the New Deal was not that states and individuals lost autonomy under a web of bureaucratic social welfare programs but rather that "capitalism still remained intact."[6] "Corporate profit" was the motive behind America's entrance into World War II.[7]

Zinn portrays religion—Christianity in particular—as a tool of the oppressors to maintain their power.[8] We read that "control of women" by means of the family was an "ingeniously effective" device of oppression because the state did not even have to get involved.[9] "Marriage enchained, and children doubled the chains," he announces, and the "illegalization of abortion clearly worked against the poor."[10] The glory of the Iroquois society prior to the arrival of the Europeans was that children were taught "not to submit to overbearing authority."[11]

Zinn scoffs at any link between free-market principles and America's prosperity. He ridicules any connection between our Christian heritage and our nation's freedom. These principles, in fact, are what he finds so egregiously offensive. His view of our history is radically different from the eyewitness testimony of one who actually studied early America firsthand. After his celebrated tour of America in 1831–32, Alexis de Tocqueville did not write of the oppression of women—just to choose one clear example. Rather, he said, "I have nowhere seen woman occupying a loftier position."[12] Our glory has become a cause for scorn.

Broadcasting from the Ivory Tower

Lest we dismiss Dr. Zinn as a fringe fanatic, we should take note of the extent of his popularity and influence. This is a man who has sold over a million copies of *A People's History* alone—not counting his other eighteen works. In August 2004, this textbook was the 141st best-selling book of any kind in America on Amazon.com. It was the fourth best-selling book at the University of Arizona, the number one book at Wesleyan University, and number seven at the University of Washington—just to name some of the schools listed on the Amazon site.

In every one of the schools mentioned, Zinn's Marxist review of U.S. history was the top-selling textbook. Popular novels and how-to books on writing dissertations were ranked higher in some cases. At the University of Arizona, Michael Moore's screed against President Bush, *Dude, Who Stole My Country?* edged out Zinn's text by a narrow margin for third place. Other colleges and universities that include Zinn's writings in their syllabi are University of Florida ("Survey of American Literature 1865–2000"), University of Massachusetts at Lowell ("U.S. History Since 1877"), Western Michigan University ("Black American Literature"), Suffolk University ("American Political Thought"), Hampton University ("The Sociology of Social Movements"), University of Massachusetts at Amherst ("Introduction to Women's Studies"), Evergreen State College ("Political Economy of Noam Chomsky"), Virginia

Tech ("Writing through Cross-Cultural Contact"), University of Illinois at Chicago (part of the General Texts for the Fulbright American Studies Institute), State University New York at Cortland ("Philosophical Issues: Prejudice and Discrimination"), University of Notre Dame ("Radical Social Thought"), University of Wisconsin at Oshkosh ("History of American Public Address"), and Berea College ("U.S. Traditions: Perspectives of the Excluded and Marginal").[13] This list is far from exhaustive.

Zinn has a B.A. from New York University and a master's and doctorate from Columbia University. He did a postdoctoral fellowship at Harvard, filled a chair at Spelman College's History Department, taught political science at Boston University for over twenty years, accepted visiting professorships at the University of Paris and the University of Bologna, and still maintains his ties with BU as a professor *emeritus*.

But his influence and popularity go far beyond these schools. Zinn has been on an antiwar lecture circuit ever since the United States responded to the war on terror in September 2001. He speaks to packed-out audiences with the faculty and administration of the college not only in attendance but usually organizing and paying for his appearance. Just a few of the universities and colleges he has lectured at since 2001 include Kansas State, University of Oregon, Denison University, University of Houston, Minnesota State, Oregon State, Fordham University, University of Wisconsin at Madison, Rutgers, Hobart and William Smith Colleges, University of South Florida, University of San Diego, Carnegie Mellon, and College of the Holy Cross.

Like Zinn, professors from elite academic colleges with their multiple degrees and vast life experiences are automatically viewed as possessing legitimacy and expertise.

And few are shy about using this platform to broadcast their views to students and the public as a whole.

As emphasized in the last chapter, elite education—whether we like it or not—is one of the chief doorways to power and influence in our modern world. Not only do they eagerly convey their message through their students who later assume these positions of leadership, but these professors also directly influence the daily workings of government, as decision makers, candidates, and news outlets look to academia for advice and commentary. When conservatives want to fill a panel of academic witnesses for a congressional hearing, the task is difficult and the list is short. Liberals have their pick of top scholars from top universities.

The "ivory tower" of academia may have formerly implied "an attitude of retreat," as one dictionary describes the term, but such is no longer the case.[14] Academics are often busy activists. For example, Sarah Weddington, who argued for a woman's "right to choose" to kill her unborn child in *Roe v. Wade*, has long been active in academic circles. She currently teaches "Gender-Based Discrimination" and "Leadership in America" at her alma mater, the University of Texas at Austin.[15] Yale graduate, George Chauncey, who was the mastermind behind the Supreme Court amicus brief that formed the "heart" of the pro-homosexual decision *Lawrence v. Texas*, is a faculty member at the University of Chicago.[16]

People with qualifications like Howard Zinn can do what he does: give talks at countless high schools, universities, and organizations across America, have multiple interviews on National Public Radio and PBS, participate in symposiums and lecture series, and get their articles published. Zinn even had to hire an agency to handle his speaking engagement requests. The agency begins his bio with words that appear frequently in the public relations flyers that colleges distribute before his appearances:

> Acclaimed historian, political theorist, teacher, storyteller and author of the legendary book *A People's History of the United States*, Howard Zinn is America's pre-eminent, most respected and best-loved radical historian.[17]

(Given his constant harping on the oppressive, wealthy elite, it seems ironic that the agency would also note that his fee range is $5,001–$10,000 per engagement.) Typical announcements read like that of Manchester College: "His *People's History of the United States* has been called 'a book that should be read by every American, student or otherwise, who wants to understand his country, its true history, and its hope for the future.'"[18] Students receive credit for attending.[19]

When "true history," according to the so-called experts, means that the framers of the Constitution were greedy elitist oppressors and the "hope for the future" of America means socialism, something is terribly wrong. Howard Zinn's America would embrace a "truly progressive income tax to diminish the huge gap between rich and poor," spent on such things as free universal health care.[20] What else would these taxes be used for? For one, they would subsidize the arts, including art that is, in Zinn's words, "outrageous, maybe politically or culturally, because it maybe involves nudity or lesbianism or in some way is offensive to those people who are still living in another century. By another century I don't mean the 21st century. I mean the 14th."[21] Taxes would not be spent on "stupid things, like nuclear weapons" or other forms of national defense.[22] His America embraces a definition of the family that subverts God's design and openly nurtures rebellion in children. His America would despise Christianity.

Is it a mere coincidence that Zinn taught for twenty years at Boston University and that Massachusetts was the first state to legalize same-sex marriage? Surely he cannot take sole credit (or blame) for this decision, but there is no doubt that he and other professors like him helped to create the intellectual climate where such a decision was not merely possible but was a foregone conclusion. Ideas do have consequences.

A recent book was published entitled *In Praise of Our Teachers: A Multicultural Tribute to Those Who Inspired Us.* The title shows how ubiquitous the worship of diversity has become in education circles. A book cannot even be written about the importance of teachers in the lives of children without throwing in the word *multicultural* to signal the fact that these stories are politically correct in every way.

This book is significant for a different reason. It clearly shows the impact of the philosophies of teachers in shaping the values of future leaders. For example, the former far-left candidate for the Democratic nomination for President and cofounder of the National Organization for Women, Shirley Chisholm, writes to extol the impact that her political science professor had in shaping her political philosophy.[23] Outspoken radical Communist and Black Panther Angela Davis, who is now a professor herself in the "history of con-sciousness" program at UC Santa Cruz, describes the awe and admiration she had for one of her teachers at Brandeis University.[24] This professor also did more than teach; he shaped a philosophy of radicalism. Marian Wright Edelman, founder and president of the liberal Children's Defense Fund, names Howard Zinn as her hero during her days as a student at Spelman College.[25] She writes that even though she first "felt shock" when Zinn declared to his class that he did not believe in Jesus Christ, she grew to learn through him that, in fact, "goodness comes in many faiths and forms."[26]

Zinn may believe that goodness comes in many faiths and forms, but on the vast majority of college campuses, there is a *de facto* rule of exclusion. Those who are political or religious conservatives are not included in the mix of faculty in anything that approximates their relative numbers in society. "Multicultural" and "diversity" cannot be translated literally in this context. As we are about to see, they mean "leftist."

Uniform Diversity

Recent days have witnessed a growing awareness of academia's ideological one-sidedness. Despite the fact that diversity has become the *sine qua non* of universities, conservatives are finally waking up and setting out to prove that they—not racial minorities, women, or gay, lesbian, bisexual, and transgendered individuals—comprise the class of people who feel the cruel effects of discrimination on most American campuses.

A rash of groups, studies, articles, books, and Web sites have emerged to expose the radical uniformity which has gripped higher education at the very moment it trumpets its diversity. Accuracy in Academia says that it exists to "return [colleges and universities] to [their] traditional mission—the quest for truth" by publicizing incidents of bias and indoctrination in its newsletter, *Campus Report*.[27] Students for Academic Freedom bear the motto, "You can't get a good education if they're only telling you half the story."[28] Ben Shapiro, a recent graduate of UCLA, wrote the book *Brainwashed: How Universities Indoctrinate America's Youth* to chronicle a myriad of shocking incidents from across the states as well as from his own alma mater.

Even Congress is starting to take note. Nearly forty cosponsors introduced a concurrent resolution in the House "expressing the sense of Congress that American colleges and universities should adopt an Academic Bill of Rights to secure the intellectual independence of faculty members and students and to protect the principle of intellectual diversity."[29] On the Senate side, the Health, Education, Labor, and Pensions Committee held a hearing entitled, "Is Intellectual Diversity an Endangered Species on America's College Campuses?"[30] Witnesses answered with a resounding, "Yes." They gave examples of conservative speakers being excluded from campus, tolerance speech codes and training sessions that prohibit any criticism of immoral lifestyles, one-sided panels and teach-ins, politicized instruction and tenure requirements, and disappearing core curricula—all aimed to silence, bully, and indoctrinate anyone who disagrees with the Left's philosophy. The opponents of the Left are silenced with epithets of "bigot," "racist," "sexist," and "homophobe" for simply holding a different view from the radical Left on issues like affirmative action or same-sex marriage.

You have probably heard these kinds of summary descriptions before. Are these exaggerations? Is the worldview in academia really that bad? Decide for yourself:

- Harvard University, long considered one of the best of the best in higher education, offers literally dozens of courses with titles such as "Body Image in French Visual Culture: 18th and 19th Century," "Gay Marriage and Families," and "Gender and Sexuality: Comparative Historical Studies of Islamic Middle East, North Africa, and South Asia."[31]

- *The Chronicle of Higher Education* published articles by professors who—less than a month after the September 11th attacks—responded to America's war against terrorists by arguing that we are the guilty ones. American history is "shot through with violence and terror," they contended, adding, "On the way home," international police should "pick up [former Secretary of State and National Security Advisor] Henry Kissinger" after Osama bin Laden.[32]

- The forty-five-thousand member American Association of University Professors (AAUP) elected as its Secretary General a former State University of New York (SUNY) president, Roger Bowen. Bowen was elected because he was a recognized champion of academic freedom. What had he done to earn this reputation? Bowen gave a thumbs-up to the school's 1997 sponsorship of the conference "Revolting Behavior," which featured workshops such as "Sex Toys for Women" and "Safe, Sane and Consensual S&M: An Alternate Way of Loving."[33] He continued to defend these open promotions of perversion in the face of criticism. Thus, he was the perfect choice to represent the largest association of college professors in the country. All parents and donors to colleges need to let the impact of this one fact sink in. The man—excuse me, my gendered speech is showing—the professor chosen to generally represent college professors was selected for the very reason that he defended the right of college teachers to teach perversion in explicit detail.

- Robert Brandon, chairman of the philosophy department at Duke University, told a newspaper, "We try to hire the best, smartest people available. . . . If, as John

36

Stuart Mill said, 'stupid people are generally conservative, then there are lots of conservatives we will never hire.'"[34] Why would he say such a thing? Duke had been criticized for hiring only leftist professors. Duke would not hire unintelligent people to be professors, and if you are politically conservative, you are by definition intellectually unqualified to teach.

What else do we see? While the vast majority of professors, particularly at prestigious schools, may not be as left-wing as Howard Zinn, the difference is more of degree than kind. *American Enterprise* was not joking when it described today's colleges and universities as "virtual one-party states, ideological monopolies, badly balanced ecosystems. They are utterly flightless birds with only one wing to flap. They do not, when it comes to political and cultural ideas, look like America."[35] TAE Research searched voter registration records and reported the following political party affiliations of professors:

- At Cornell University, the departments of anthropology, economics, English, history, political science, psychology, sociology, and women's studies are composed of 166 members of parties of the Left, while only 6 are members of parties of the Right.
- At Harvard University, the economics, political science, and sociology departments have 25 Left-leaning professors for every 1 on the Right.
- The University of California at Los Angeles (UCLA) features 141 Democratic, Green, or Working Families Party members versus a total of 9 Republicans or Libertarians in departments comparable to those above.
- Stanford University is little better. Here TAE found 151 Left professors in such departments as economics,

English, history, political science, and sociology and 17 who registered in a party of the Right.

- Across the board, the ratio is skewed: 54–3 at Brown University, 59–10 at Penn State, 94–15 at the University of Texas at Austin, 35–1 at SUNY at Binghamton, 72–1 at UC Santa Barbara, 116–5 at the University of Colorado at Boulder, and 59–10 at the University of Maryland.[36]

In this context it makes perfect sense when school presidents like Stephen Trachtenberg of George Washington University inform graduating seniors during commencement ceremonies, "If anybody has a mortarboard, you can move your tassels from right to left, right to left, which is what I hope happened to your politics in the last four years."[37] This is what we call fair and balanced instruction? Probably, according to the university spokesman, who maintained, "His politics are known, I would say, but I don't think he's trying to impose them on anybody."[38]

Speaking of commencement ceremonies, well-known radical-turned-conservative David Horowitz oversaw a study that compiled a record of graduation speakers from the past ten years at thirty-two elite colleges and universities. The numbers are disconcerting. Twenty-two schools of the thirty-two listed failed to feature a single conservative or Republican individual.[39] Instead, Tom Brokaw and George Stephanopolous took the stage at Columbia University; Al Gore, Madeleine Albright, and Daniel Patrick Moynihan gave addresses at Harvard; and Janet Reno did the same at Berkeley.[40]

The *Washington Times* observed the trend when it reported the results of a poll of Ivy League professors conducted by Luntz Research Companies.[41] What did it reveal?

Forty percent of these professors said that they support slavery reparations (a radical theory that today's white-owned businesses need to pay damages to blacks because their distant relatives were slaves), while 74 percent oppose a national missile defense system.[42] Their favorite American president from the past forty years is none other than Bill Clinton.[43] Zero percent name the Christian Coalition as an organization they would identify with, while 44 percent say that the ACLU most closely matches their views.[44]

In regard to economic issues, Gallup concluded that 67 percent of Americans wanted some of their money returned to them in the form of a tax cut during 2002, but Luntz found that only 13 percent of Ivy League professors did.[45] A full 80 percent oppose using tax cuts to deal with a federal surplus in any given year.[46]

Ivy League professors are out of touch with America, and they are proud of it. When I was in law school, Gonzaga University hired Harvard's professor of constitutional law, Paul Freund, to teach a one-semester version of the course that I took. One day I was visiting with Professor Freund in his office when the conversation drifted to some political topic. He remarked, "It's too bad that we make decisions in America by counting heads rather than by weighing them."

It was a practiced remark representing his true feelings. Conservatives are too uneducated and dim-witted to be allowed to vote correctly. We should have a government by the liberal elite rather than a representative democracy.

When they are recruiting students or soliciting donations, most universities are smart enough to keep their radicalism under wraps. However, one does not need to dig very far to see what is really going on. Listen to the words of long-time Harvard professor Duncan Kennedy, who encouraged fellow faculty members across the land: "In addition to supporting leftist students, we can undermine the complacent centrism of countless other students."[47] Kennedy's remarks were not whispered in secret but were openly published in a scholarly journal for all to read.

The academic Left attacks traditional values on several fronts. No trail is more worn than the attack on a belief in the God of the Bible.

Teaching without God

If the fear of God is the beginning of wisdom and knowledge of the Holy One is understanding, then most elite university professors cannot lay claim to much of either. Many echo Alan Dershowitz, the well-known, Yale-educated, Harvard Law School professor and civil liberties lawyer, who wrote in a *Harvard Crimson* op-ed that "indeed, it is at least as likely that space aliens exist as it is that God exists. The former is, however, a scientifically testable hypothesis (at least in theory); whereas the latter—for at least most theologians—is not."[48]

We might laugh at such a statement if it were not so pitiful. Even more sobering are the diatribes against God recorded by *Brainwashed* author Ben Shapiro in his chapter entitled, "The War on God." Stanford University's John McCarthy does not hesitate to say that "the evidence on the god question is in a similar state to the evidence on the werewolf question. So I am an atheist."[49] Another prominent academic, ethicist Peter Singer of Princeton University, asks, "If we don't play God, who will? There seem to me to be three possibilities: there is a God, but He doesn't care about evil and suffering; there is a God who cares, but He or She is a bit of an underachiever; or there is no God. Personally, I believe the latter."[50]

When God is absent, neither absolute truth nor virtue can survive. A study commissioned by the National Association of Scholars and conducted by Zogby International reports that 73 percent of college seniors surveyed claim that their professors taught them that "what is right and wrong depends on differences in individual values and cultural diversity."[51] These same seniors also decided that "recruiting a diverse workforce in which women and minorities are advanced and promoted" is a more important business practice than "providing clear and accurate business statements to stockholders and creditors"—by a 15-percent margin.[52] Nevertheless, the students seem unaware that this should cause a problem. Ninety-seven percent agreed (most said "strongly") that their college studies were "preparing [them] to behave ethically in [their] future professional life."[53]

These numbers gain even more credibility when we read actual examples of teachers' words. Michigan State University professor, Ron Puhek, wrote in his book *Mind, Soul, and Spirit: An Inquiry into the Spiritual Derailments of Modern Life*:

> From our perspective, we are the standard that creates the world. We are the absolute. . . . Despite all this relativity of knowledge and being, we must avoid the temptation of the twentieth century. We must not assert absolute relativism. Not only is that assertion a logical absurdity, it is experientially invalid. Truth does force us to conclude that all things are relative.[54]

"Absolute relativism" is a "logical absurdity" but "truth does force us to conclude that all things are relative." When reading these laughable contradictions side by side, one is reminded of the character Professor Kirke in C. S. Lewis's *Chronicles of Narnia*, crying out, "Logic! What are they teaching in the schools these days?"

Elizabeth Kiss, director of the Kenan Ethics Program at Duke University and associate professor of political science, said the following in an interview at the University of Maryland: "Some say that . . . ethics is more a matter of invention than of discovery, and we don't call inventions 'true' or 'false.' I think it's a fascinating question whether ethics is invented, discovered, or a mixture of the two."[55] This is how she advocates "teaching character in college." When a leading professor of ethics can only say that the existence of an unalterable standard revealing right and wrong is merely a "fascinating question," it is easy to understand why the dominant majority of college graduates have embraced the idea of situational ethics.

The outcome of these philosophies is illustrated nowhere more effectively than in professors' attitudes concerning sexual morality.

When Evil Is Called Good

Given the disregard for God and truth outlined above, it should come as little surprise when Elizabeth Bartholet, who has been a professor of civil rights and family law at Harvard since the 1970s, describes the "gayby boom" video *Daddy & Papa* with the words, "A poignant, compelling story of gay fathers in today's America as they parent across racial, national, and religious lines, yet personify the most fundamental of family values. A winner of a film that I would like to make universally required viewing."[56] Bartholet believes in neither "family values" nor freedom since she is willing to force everyone to watch such homosexual propaganda.

The academic world is certainly not shocked by Professor Paul Robinson, who attended both Harvard and Yale and is a professor of humanities at Stanford. His self-proclaimed research interests include psychoanalysis, "history of ideas about human sexuality, especially the experience of gays and lesbians," and "the connection between intellectual history and the history of opera."[57] Robinson has even written a book called *Gay Lives: Homosexual Autobiography from John Addington Symonds to Paul Monette*, which his daughter lightheartedly calls "academic porn."[58] If we had any lingering doubt concerning his thoughts on biblical morality, a Stanford colleague would assure us that Robinson is "fascinated by sex and is a constant, funny critic of puritanism."[59]

This is not unusual. Yale offers a class called "Sex and Gender as Performance." The course description announces that students will participate in an "examination of corporeal erotics informing contemporary film, club music, dance, performance art, and photography."[60] It continues, getting a little more specific, and says that there will be a "focus on body works by Ethyl Eichelberger, Lyle Ashton Harris, Todd Haynes, Janet and Michael Jackson, Bill T. Jones, Madonna, Ultra Naté, RuPaul, and Todd Solondz."[61] Yale, by the way, no longer requires students to study American history.[62] Eliminating such "archaic" requirements leaves time for courses where the pursuit of raw sexuality earns academic credit.

Yes, we should shudder. When teachers at our nation's most influential institutions of higher education can spend time and money on vile trivia, we must recognize that future leaders will lack both substance and goodness.

Homosexual influence is so pervasive in academia that even explicitly Christian schools are not immune. Calvin College in Michigan, a member of the Christian College Coalition, has a mission statement that describes the school as one that conforms to the "Reformed tradition of historic Christianity." It seeks to be an "agent of renewal in the academy, church, and society," and pledges "fidelity to Jesus Christ, offering our hearts and lives to do God's work in God's world."[63] Yet, even so, the College's Broene Counseling Center hosts a discussion group for gay and lesbian students. If you think that the goal of the group is gently to urge these wayward sheep back into the fold, you are mistaken. It is exactly the opposite. "Our purpose," Calvin's Web site says, "is to provide a safe place where gay and lesbian students can 'carry each other's burdens . . .' (Gal. 6:2). Sad to say, amidst the societal ignorance, hatred, and fear of gay persons, we feel the need to protect their identities as well as their meeting place."[64]

Read this account from Calvin's student newspaper and decide for yourself how faithful to historic Christianity Calvin really is:

> Last Thursday in the Heyns basement, three
> gay students spoke to a crowd of around two hun-
> dred students about their experiences at Calvin.
> The student panel, consisting of Justin Jager, Janee
> Harvey and Peter Fortner, was the first of its kind
> in Calvin's history.
>
> The discussion they led on Thursday night was
> the third and final installment of the second annual
> late-night series about homosexuality held at BHT.
> Tuesday night's discussion featured Rev. Jack
> Roeda, the minister of Church of the Servant, who

spoke about how the church should respond to gays according to the 1973 Synod guidelines.

Thursday night's dialogue [was] led by three openly gay students. The students shared their stories of coming out and how this has affected their lives as Christians and as students at Calvin. In so doing, they hoped to facilitate communication between straight and gay students and to let other gay students know that they are not alone.

The three students who led the discussion are participants in the Calvin Gay and Lesbian Discussion Group and made an open offer to speak on campus. Josh Armstrong, the Resident Director of BHT who organized a gay debate last year, responded to this offer.

It was emphasized throughout the discussion that the purpose of the night was not to engage in a theological debate over the issue of homosexuality. Rather, the students wanted to show that the debate involves real people. Harvey said that their purpose was "not to win some sort of proof text competition, but to share with others what we have experienced and to hear the stories of others, both gay and straight."

Jill Eelkema, a student who attended the Thursday night discussion, appreciated that the Gay Debate II was not really a debate. "I was glad that the main focus was on the care that we can give each other, not on the theological issues involved. More than being a theologically based school, Calvin is a community of Christians who need to support each other more than they do now," she said.[65]

Did you see any evidence that these Calvin students uphold the Bible as the standard of truth? Experience—both gay and straight—defines truth at least to these particular people at Calvin College. Remember, the College itself offers all of this material to the world at large on its official Web site.

According to this self-described Christian school and multitudes of secular ones, whether one should embrace homosexuality is entirely up for grabs. No, more than that—expressions of homosexual behavior are good. It is progress.

Progressing Backward

For far too many professors, views like Paul Robinson's and George Chauncey's are not at all repulsive. Instead, they might be called "progressive." This seems to be something of a code word among left-of-the-left college professors. "Liberal" simply does not go far enough.

"Progressivism," in the words of NYU School of Law professor Peggy Cooper Davis, "entails commitments to social welfare, anti-subordination, and civic empowerment."[66] She goes on to call the Supreme Court justices of *Planned Parenthood v. Casey* "centrists" when they affirmed a right to an abortion and wrote, "at the heart of liberty is the right to define one's own concept of existence, of meaning, of the universe, and of the mystery of human life."[67] She also reveals what she means by "anti-subordination" in another article when she decries the bigotry of conservatives who are determined "to enforce a moral vision in which abortion and homosexual intimacy are intolerable crimes."[68] Her moral vision, like that of other progressives, pronounces each of these practices as an unqualified good.

A "pro-family, progressive political coalition" was the agenda that Jennifer Hochschild set out to promote at an event sponsored by The Century Foundation in 2000.[69] Her impressive *curriculum vitae* lists only three places of employment over the past thirty years: Duke, Princeton, and Harvard Universities. Her affiliations lend her ideas tremendous legitimacy in the eyes of many.[70] The gathering also featured Theda Skocpol, a fellow progressive and a faculty member at Harvard University. After Skocpol spelled out the tenets of a "working family social policy" that included universal health care, "child support assurance," and paid family leave, Hochschild made the following points:

- "Survey opinion data show that citizens continue to vote in their financial self-interest—if voters do not have a direct stake in progressive policies, they might be unwilling to support tax increases."
- "In the future, if there is an economic downturn, the public may be less willing to pay for expansive policies (existing ones or those under consideration) for working families."
- "American politics are still dominated by an ethic of individual responsibility, creating an impediment to liberal social welfare programs."[71]

We must slow down and reread that last quotation. Belief in "individual responsibility" impedes the Left from promoting more "social welfare programs." Why would any parent want their son or daughter taught by sworn enemies of individual responsibility? Why would any for-profit company give a single dime to a college that tears at responsibility in order to promulgate more welfare? (This also brings to mind legitimate questions about the emphasis on group projects in lieu of independent work at all levels of academic instruction.)

It is antiprogressive for families to be so dogged in their determination to take the initiative in providing for their own needs. It is progressive to have the government take money from some families and give it to others. Unsurprisingly, Hochschild wrote in a *Newsday* article that the tax cuts initiated by the Bush administration "would be laughable if it were not so pernicious."[72] Tax increases— along with homosexual marriage—are now the hallmarks of the "pro-family" policy popular among the academic elite.

A tax cut is not the only thing that professors have labeled "pernicious." America itself falls into this category too.

Loathing the Colossus

Howard Zinn enlightened a crowd of Harvard students in December 2003 with the statements, "The history of American occupation is not a pretty history. . . . It is a history of cruelty and violence. . . . Bush, Saddam Hussein, Bin Ladin, they are all terrorists."[73] Similar sentiments were shared by faculty who participated in the Yale-sponsored teach-in on Iraq. One brave classics professor denounced the event "for its utter failure to include a single spokesman in favor of military action."[74] Professors at Columbia University held another antiwar teach-in on March 27, 2003 that caused one student to lament that it was simply a "fervid presentation of an exclusive viewpoint . . . where professors could express their viewpoints unopposed."[75] That solitary perspective was summed up in the statement, "I'm not sure which is more frightening: the horror that engulfed New York City or the apocalyptic rhetoric emanating daily from the White House."[76]

Just pause and think about that one. The academic elite at Columbia University cannot decide whether the attacks on New York City on September 11 are worse than speeches by President George W. Bush decrying the terrorist attacks. What possible basis can there be for such moral confusion? One is the mass murder of thousands of Americans through a cowardly act of unannounced war. The other is political speech that leftists don't agree with. Calling America to a patriotic and strong military response against terror can only be morally wrong if America is morally indefensible. Such remarks at Columbia show how deeply rooted the hatred of America really is in such circles.

Author Daniel J. Flynn, in his book *Why the Left Hates America: Exposing the Lies That Have Obscured Our Nation's Greatness*, perceptively points out that the roots of today's anti-American sentiments lie in four primary movements: Communism, relativism, Cultural Marxism and the New Left, and multiculturalism.[77] These roots have grown deep on most college campuses, producing citizen-leaders who cannot decide whether our nation is worth defending.

There once was a time when part of the purpose of education in America was to equip citizens with the tools they needed to govern themselves in liberty and responsibility. It was not to silence criticism—quite the contrary. Somehow professors today seem to exalt what they call "dissent" as a higher and more noble good than any display of patriotism. Flynn sums up this phenomenon as follows:

> Stephen Decatur, a naval hero of the War of 1812, famously toasted: "Our country! In her intercourse with foreign nations, may she always be in the right, but our country, right or wrong." To this,

the American Left mindlessly retorts: Our country,
she is always wrong.[78]

Now in American institutions of higher education, flag-
burning seems more preferable to the Star-Spangled Banner's
display. One state school forbid students from adorning their
walls with patriotic pictures after the September 11 attacks
"because they were offending people."[79] The *Wall Street
Journal* gives us the following synopsis of a typical "peace
rally," this one held at Brown University:

> At Brown University, some 120 students walked
> out of class Tuesday to protest America's efforts to
> defend itself against terrorism. *The Brown Daily
> Herald* reports that "Some professors, including John
> Tomasi, associate professor of political science, and
> William Keach, professor of English, let their classes
> out early so students could attend the protest. At one
> point, Keach took the microphone and said, "What
> happened on Sept. 11th was terrorism, but what
> happened during the Gulf War was also
> terrorism." We'd like to think he's referring to Iraq's
> invasion of Kuwait, but we somehow doubt it.[80]

Attendees played along. One told a reporter, "I was cheering
when the Pentagon got hit because I know about the brutal-
ity of the military. The American flag is nothing but a
symbol of hate and should be used for toilet paper for all
I care."[81] Crude anti-American remarks hardly stop there.
University of New Mexico professor Richard Berthold informed his students, "Anyone who can blow up the Pentagon
gets my vote."[82]

Faculty members and students like those at Duke and
Tufts Universities were harassed and disciplined for daring
to show support for our military. One professor had his

Web site removed because it contained links to articles that supported the use of force against terrorism.[83] One student joined others in displaying "God Bless America" on a cannon decorated with patriotic colors in October 2001 and was summarily attacked by bandanna-covered members of the university's "Coalition for Social Justice and Nonviolence."[84] Tufts excused the attackers without reprimand.[85] Social justice and nonviolence? Evidently, on these campuses, America is the enemy; the September 11th terrorists are the heroes. In the words of one UC Berkeley professor, "What goes around comes around. . . . They aren't cowards, if nothing else, it surely isn't cowardly to ride the plane in for something you believe."[86]

Similarly, professors at Princeton tried to help their students cope with the tragedy by blaming America's past. Dean Michael Rothschild of the University's Woodrow Wilson School comforted them with the words, "There is a terrible and understandable desire to find and punish whoever was responsible for this. But as we think about it, it's very important for Americans to think about our own history."[87] Professor Emeritus Richard Falk likewise explained, "Democracies, because they have a sense of self-pride and moral consciousness, can often act without restraint and be destructive of the values they are trying to promote. . . . there needs to be an understanding of why this kind of suicidal violence could be undertaken against our country."[88]

This attitude is commonplace. As a faculty member of Yale's history department queried, "Suppose that there existed today a powerful, unified Arab-Muslim state that stretched from Algeria to Turkey and Arabia. In those conditions, would not many Americans steadily grow to loathe that colossus?"[89] In his mind a fundamentalist Islamic state that tortures nonadherents is not qualitatively different from a representative democracy. Is it the mere territorial size of America that justifies the Arab world in hating us so much? Is there no difference between a constitutional republic with freedom for all and Muslim dictatorial regimes with no meaningful respect for human rights? One can reasonably guess that a professor who had lived under such a regime would understand the difference between free America and a state where dissenters have their tongues cut out and are paraded around to inspire fear if they express such animus toward its leaders—just as Saddam Hussein did to one Iraqi man before America stepped in.[90]

Let me be clear. I am not saying that such professors should be silenced by violence or otherwise. I am merely saying that they are wrong and, perhaps, that no one in their right mind should send their children or money to such institutions.

Avoiding the Mind-Set of Grasshoppers

The academic giants are indeed formidable foes. Their strongholds are entrenched. Yet, as we continue to survey their presence in the land, it should not be a cause for fear or retreat. If we see only the giants and the philosophies that gave them birth, we are missing the point. The land began with good fruit. We have before us the opportunity to see with eyes of faith—hope in the power of God and His redeeming grace. Let us not be like the spies who were sent to wander in the wilderness for forty years after weeping, "There also we saw the Nephilim . . . and we became like grasshoppers in our own sight, and so we were in their sight" (Num. 13:33 NASB).

Contrary to popular university teaching, America is not, was not, and has not always been the most oppressive place on the face of the earth. Certainly, we must begin from a position of brokenness over the twisted truth and wickedness that now dwells in our land, for that is where healing begins. Yet there is a resilient beauty in our nation's past that can guide our future.

CHAPTER 4

The Way We Weren't: Ivy League Attacks on American History

In 1986, the Supreme Court of the United States upheld the right of states to ban homosexual conduct in the case of *Bowers v. Hardwick*.[1] I was the coauthor of an amicus brief in that case that examined the history of antisodomy laws at the time of the adoption of the Bill of Rights and the Fourteenth Amendment. The Court used our brief, quoting from it nearly word for word in some of its footnotes.

In 2003, the Court reversed that decision in *Lawrence v. Texas*.[2] Again, I was the coauthor of another amicus brief discussing the history of such laws. The task we faced in writing our brief this time, however, was far more challenging. We were confronted with the briefs of numerous professors of history who contended that the history relied upon in Bowers was grossly inaccurate.

They argued that private acts of homosexuality were actually welcomed in the early days of our Republic. The only punishments were for public acts, crimes against minors, and acts committed by force.

After reading these briefs, I actually laughed out loud. I simply could not believe that any credible judge would believe these claims in light of clear, repeated statements made by lawmakers and judges who decried sodomy as a "crime against nature" that was not worthy of further description by civilized nations.

I was wrong about the historical gullibility of the justices of the Supreme Court. They fully embraced these absurd theories of this cadre of history professors in the face of incontrovertible facts from original sources. Of course, the Court desired to reach the pro-homosexual outcome, so its decision has no weight in deciding who had more correctly discerned the truths of our past.

This kind of fanciful history turns out to be standard fare in many history courses in America's elite colleges. My experience in the Supreme Court reveals the true nature of today's history courses: they offer thinly disguised political advocacy of a particular viewpoint antithetical to both the facts and the philosophy of the American founding. "History is past politics, and politics present history" is a famous saying that is only partially correct.[3] We would have to add that history classes are the *future* of politics as well.

One history textbook from the early nineteenth century posited, "To consider history only as a magazine of facts, arranged in the order of their dates, is nothing more than the indulgence of a vain and childish curiosity, a study which tends to no valuable or useful purpose."[4] Professors today understand and practice this principle well. This textbook continues, however, "The object of the study of history is one of the noblest of the pursuits of man. It is to furnish the mind with the knowledge of that great art on which depends the existence, the preservation, the happiness and prosperity of states and empires. That the connection of politics with morality is inseparable, the smallest acquaintance with history is sufficient to show."[5]

This view of the interconnectedness of politics, history, and objective morality is entirely foreign to most historians today. Do not misunderstand. Today's teachers of history see a connection—but one in which the good guys and the bad guys are essentially reversed.

From our exposé of Howard Zinn in the last chapter, we already know that history has taken a turn for the worse on America's college campuses. Until we take a closer look at the Left's strongholds in this field, however, we have only a faint idea of how far down this destructive path professors have traveled.

To the leftist educator, history presents a prime opportunity to reinforce the themes we have illustrated thus far. For example, since diversity functions as the ultimate *sine qua non*, the virtues of all cultures past and present must be extolled, with one exception. Western civilization and all of its "misogynist, gay-bashing" tendencies is hopelessly corrupt, and it must be condemned for its "hatred and selfishness." As we recall from Howard Zinn's history, the Iroquois tribal culture represented the epitome of decency and equality, while the authors of America's Bill of Rights were more akin to avaricious capitalist pigs.

There is another reason Western civilization is viewed as regressive in the minds of many history professors today. In sum, it has dared to suggest that basic human rights derive from the hand of God. Religion—particularly religion that asserts any kind of absolute standard, such as Christianity—appears to this cadre of academics to be the archenemy of liberty. M. Stanton Evans in *The Theme Is Freedom* describes "the liberal history lesson" in these terms:

Freedom, democracy and intellectual inquiry allegedly flourished in the pagan era, only to be crushed to earth in the Christian Middle Ages. This regime of clerical oppression supposedly ended when "humanist" scholars of the Renaissance and Enlightenment threw off the shackles of religion, rediscovered the learning of the ancients, and set modernity on the path to freedom. It appears to follow that a regime of liberty requires a secularist, anticlerical view of religious questions.[6]

Hence, it is natural for these historians to name Emma Goldman (an American anarchist who worked to help the Russian revolution) and Margaret Sanger (the founder of Planned Parenthood) as heroes[7] rather than men like George Washington and others of the founding generation. The latter are instead portrayed exclusively as "slave-holders, Indian-killers, and militarists."[8] New England witch hunts are highlighted by some professors as if the legacy of the Puritans consists entirely of fanatical bigotry and unenlightened suppression of dissent.[9] The heroes are those who advocated the separation of God and state *in toto*.

Leftist history professors are anything but shy, retiring scholars; they are street-savvy political activists. They file amicus briefs showing how "the institution of marriage has absorbed many changes," thus making history a convenient tool for winning points in the gay rights debate.[10] They present themselves as stalwart defenders of the Constitution in their effort to lambaste the National Rifle Association and challenge the effort to impeach Bill Clinton. And finally, every decent history department at elite universities has more than its share of militant anti-war activists. It is common for these individuals to be the same ones who are pro-Arab, anti-Israel, and, for good measure, openly Marxist. In other words, professor and radical communist Noam Chomsky has a lot of friends in academia.

It is important to note here that the label of leftist is not intended to reduce the nature of the problem to a litany of political sins. As with disciplines other than history, our first concern should be for truth and how that truth should order our lives both as individuals and as American citizens. The various professors we will examine in this chapter may come from different philosophical positions, but a common thread is the rejection of God's revealed propositions in favor of a post-Christian, sociologically based view of reality. In *The Church at the End of the Twentieth Century*, Francis Schaeffer wrote:

> Most of us catch our presuppositions like measles. Why do people fit into the post-Christian world? I would urge that it is . . . not that the facts are against the Christian presuppositions, but simply that the Christian view is presented as unthinkable. The better the university, the better the brainwashing tends to be.[11]

History is a perfect vehicle for such tactics.

Queering Public Policy

Gay and Lesbian Advocates and Defenders (more commonly known by its acronym, GLAD) filed an amicus brief filed in the Massachusetts Supreme Judicial Court in November 2002 by "Professors of the History of Marriage, Families, and the Law."[12] The case that prompted it was *Hillary Goodridge, et al. v. Department of Public Health*.[13] The question was, in the words of the Court's Chief

Justice, Margaret Marshall, "whether, consistent with the Massachusetts Constitution, the Commonwealth may deny the protections, benefits, and obligations conferred by civil marriage to two individuals of the same sex who wish to marry." Marshall was joined by three other justices who said, "No, it may not," and Massachusetts became the first state in the Union to legalize same-sex marriage.

There is little doubt that the GLAD brief, among others, must have had some influence on the decision. If nothing else, it lent credibility to the position that civil marriage is created exclusively by the government and thus can be redefined at will, *ad infinitum*. The brief states, "That marriage remains a vital and relevant institution is a tribute to the law's ability to accommodate changing values, not the rigid adherence to rules and practices of another time. The Department of Public Health's refusal to grant marriage licenses to the gay and lesbian plaintiff couples here flouts this robust tradition." A "tradition" of "accommodating changing values," besides being somewhat of an oxymoron, is precisely the idea that the authors of the brief were trying to convey and the conclusion that a majority of the justices ultimately reached.

The lie that these historians so skillfully propagated is that granting gays and lesbians the right to receive the benefits of the marriage institution symbolizes "no radical change." "Rather," they said, "it represents the logical next step in this Court's long tradition of reforming marriage to fit the evolving nature of committed intimate relationships and the rights of the individuals in those relationships." Their argument is that men and women for centuries have simply recreated marriage as they see fit—beginning with, of all people, the early Christians. They illustrate the evolution further by trumpeting the glories of no-fault divorce, a previous step in the process. God and His standards apparently played no role in instituting marriage nor in saying what it should look like today.

Who were these historians? "We have written leading books and articles," they announce, "uncovering and analyzing the history of marriage and marriage law in the United States and in Massachusetts. This brief is submitted to assist the Court's deliberations by offering an analysis of the history of marriage law and practice in Massachusetts based on our scholarship." Scholarship is the key to a hearing, as we have seen before. This becomes even clearer when we take a look at the amici biographies in the brief's appendix.

First, there is Peter Bardaglio, who teaches history at Ithaca College and whose book *Reconstructing the Household: Families, Sex, and the Law in the Nineteenth-Century South* won the Organization of American Historians' James Rawley Prize in 1996 for the best book on race relations. Then we have Norma Basch, a professor at Rutgers, who teaches and writes on marriage, divorce, gender and women's issues, and American legal history. Law professor Richard Chused is based at Georgetown University and has likewise written prolifically on the topic of divorce and women's property law. Another law professor, Nancy Dowd of the University of Florida, had one book published entitled *Redefining Fatherhood* and another with the telling name, *In Defense of Single Parent Families*. Ariela Dubler is at Columbia University, where she teaches and writes on marriage history and "nonmarital relations." Sarah Barringer Gordon normally instructs her students at the University of Pennsylvania in religion, marriage, and gender, but at the time of the brief's filing, she was a visiting research fellow at Princeton.

Michael Grossberg not only is a prize-winning author but also the editor of the *American Historical Review* and a professor at Indiana University. Steve Mintz is on the faculty of the University of Houston and on the board of directors of the Council on Contemporary Families. His book of note is entitled *Domestic Revolutions: A Social History of American Family Life*. We also find signers from Yale, Harvard, Princeton, New York University, University of Wisconsin, University of Tulsa, University of Minnesota, University of Oregon, University of Illinois, University of Southern California, Vassar College, University of Chicago, and Cornell. Maybe the justices were just plain intimidated.

A nearly identical group of historians then descended on the United States Supreme Court in their ongoing advocacy of gay rights. The following January, "professors and scholars who teach and write about history and are knowledgeable about the history and treatment of lesbians and gay men in America" filed an amicus brief in support of a homosexual couple challenging Texas' antisodomy law. (This is the brief I refer to in the opening of this chapter.)[14]

The brief is skillfully written. It weaves together history, legal definitions of sodomy, cultural attitudes toward homosexuality, and even biblical exegesis to make the point that only in the last century has "the government [begun] to classify and discriminate against certain of its citizens on the basis of their homosexual status." The authors conclude, "In recent years, a decisive majority of Americans have recognized such measures for what they are—discrimination that offends the principles of our Nation—yet a number of them remain in place. The 1973 Texas Homosexual Conduct Law at issue is an example of such discriminatory laws. They hold no legitimate place in our Nation's traditions." Skillfully written? Yes. Accurate history? Not a chance. Rather than being welcomed in early America, the truth is made plain about the Founders' attitude toward homosexuality (buggery) by the New York law enacted in 1787—the year of the Constitutional Convention.

> That the detestable and abominable vice of bug-
> gery, committed with mankind, or beast, shall be
> from henceforth adjudged felony; and such order
> and form of process therein shall be used against
> the offenders, as in cases of felony at the common
> law; and that every person being thereof convicted,
> by verdict, confession, or outlawry, shall be hanged
> by the neck, until he or she shall be dead.
> *Laws of New York, ch. 21, p. 391 (passed February
> 14, 1787)*

The amicus that most commands our attention, however, is George Chauncey. He graduated from Yale in 1989 and has more than succeeded in making his mark on the world since that time. According to his official University of Chicago faculty bio, he has been awarded fellowships from the John Simon Guggenheim Memorial Foundation, the Cullman Center for Scholars and Writers, National Humanities Center, American Council of Learned Societies, Rutgers Center for Historical Analysis, and New York University School of Law. One of his most popular publications, *Gay New York: Gender, Urban Culture, and the Making of the Gay Male World, 1890–1940*, received the Merle Curti award from the Organization of American Historians, Los Angeles Times Book Prize, Frederick Jackson Turner Award for "the best first book in any field of history," and the Lambda Literary Award.[15]

This gives us a clue about his real claim to fame. Rick Perlstein of the *University of Chicago Magazine* does not hesitate to describe Chauncey as the historian behind *Lawrence v. Texas*. In fact, Perlstein writes that "the heart of Justice Anthony Kennedy's new legal doctrine in the 6–3 decision, ranging over some dozen paragraphs, is a virtual recapitulation of the Historian's Brief arguments," which Chauncey played a key role in constructing.[16] This new doctrine was the idea that since homosexuality never comprised a distinct category or identity under the broader umbrella of sodomy, gay men were simply not prosecuted in our nation's past. Put another way, discrimination on the basis of sexual orientation is a twentieth-century phenomenon, and thus to allow the states to continue criminalizing homosexuality is bigoted and historically un-American.

When the majority of Supreme Court justices adopted this reasoning, Perlstein wrote, "Chauncey couldn't be happier. 'I'm thrilled with the decision' [he said]—and that 'the Court took the findings of recent historical scholarship seriously.'"[17]

Other people take his historical scholarship seriously, too. Chauncey has been a featured guest at Texas A&M ("Another West Side Story? Latino Gay Culture and Urban Politics in Postwar New York City"), the University of Maryland ("*Lawrence v. Texas*: Sexual Identity/Politics in the 20th Century"), Hobart and William Smith Colleges ("The Strange Career of the Closet: Gay Culture, Consciousness, and Politics"), the University of Wisconsin ("What Matters to Me and Why"), and the University of Illinois at Urbana-Champaign ("Rethinking the Closet: Lesbian and Gay Life Before Stonewall" and "The 'Fairy' and the Prostitute: Gender, Street Culture, and Working Class Sexuality in the

Early Twentieth Century"), among others.[18] He was a distinguished guest faculty member for the "Sexuality, Theory, and Culture" Advanced Interdisciplinary Graduate Seminar at UCLA's LGBTS program and participated in the University of Minnesota's Feminist Studies Colloquium Series.[19] Columbia University and CSU Fullerton are just a couple of the schools that list his books in syllabi.[20] The University of Chicago's Department of History, where he teaches, is one of the most highly regarded in the field.

Why is he in such high demand? Chauncey's various activities are revealing. First of all, his "field specialties" consist of American social and urban history, the history of gender and sexuality (including gay history), and Cold War culture and politics. He has authored numerous books and articles with names like *The Strange Career of the Closet: Gay Culture, Consciousness, and Politics from the Second World War to the Gay Liberation Era* and "'Privacy Could Only Be Had in Public': Gay Uses of the Streets" in the book *Stud: Architectures of Masculinity*. As for his teaching career, his University of Chicago biography says:

> Professor Chauncey regularly teaches graduate courses on postwar American culture, critical studies of sexuality, and the historiography of the twentieth century. He also teaches undergraduate courses on postwar culture, urban history, and lesbian and gay history. He is the Director of the Lesbian and Gay Studies Project of the Center for Gender Studies, which organizes lecture series and conferences, provides dissertation fellowships and research grants to University of Chicago graduate students, and cosponsors the Gender and Sexuality Studies Workshop.

Chauncey does what he does for a good reason: he understands firsthand how influential a college professor can be in a student's life. One of his two "great mentors" was Yale professor John Boswell, whose 1980 book *Christianity, Social Tolerance and Homosexuality: Gay People in Western Europe from the Beginning of the Christian Era to the Fourteenth Century* was written to show that the Christian world did not until recently consider homosexuality a moral wrong. (Boswell died of AIDS over a decade ago.) A second mentor at Yale who inspired Chauncey to pursue gay scholarship was Dr. Nancy Cott.

While speaking at a University of Chicago lecture sponsored by the ACLU in early 2003, Chauncey credited Cott's *The Bonds of Womanhood: "Woman's Sphere" in New England, 1780–1835* for giving him the idea that the classes of "gay" and "straight" emerged only recently, much like the appearance of feminism in the eighteenth century defined the group of people who think that men and women hold "complementary 'separate spheres.'"[21] He has followed her footsteps in more ways than one, and he has had her blessing.

Nancy Cott is quite a figure. She left her long tenure at Yale as a specialist in women's history to go to Harvard, where she can now "explore gender from the other side" by teaching courses such as "Men, Manhood, and Masculinity."[22] She is referred to as a "founding mother" of women's studies and says that her "own interests over these 25 years or so have been very much at one with the development of the field, in moving from uncovering women and enabling the 'inarticulate' to speak to understanding that gender is operative in all spheres of political, social, cultural life."[23]

Naturally, the idea of marriage is linked to Cott's fascination with "gender." Far from condemning the idea of matrimony in her book *Public Vows: A History of Marriage and the Nation*, she exalts it. It is her definition of what it is supposed to look like, however, that should give us cause for concern. She rightly points out that in early America marriage was considered a God-given institution with civil ramifications; "republican success relied on faithfulness to monogamy" between one man who provided for and protected his wife and a woman whose virtuous company "could refine and polish."[24] (This was also the Christian ideal that college students were taught through such texts as William Paley's *The Principles of Moral and Political Philosophy* (1785), which she refers to as "the most widely read college text on the subject in the first half of the nineteenth century."[25]) Cott then proceeds to emphasize how marriage has been transformed from the idea of a "yoke" to "freedom in a chosen space."[26] In other words, as long as "consent" is involved, marriage can mean whatever individuals want it to. The government must not deny legal marriage to those who ask because the extension of this civil right only to heterosexual couples "reinforces a caste supremacy of heterosexuality over homosexuality just as laws banning marriages across the color line exhibited and reinforced white supremacy."[27] Gays and lesbians should continue to pursue their quest for equality.

Besides taking this philosophy to the courts, Cott has done her job in legislative bodies. Her testimony before the Vermont House Judiciary Committee was apparently significant enough to be included in Andrew Sullivan's book, *Same-Sex Marriage Pro & Con: A Reader*. She also shared her "historian's perspective on the evolving nature of marriage" in support of same-sex civil unions before the Joint Committee on the Judiciary of the Massachusetts legislature in October 2003. Here is her conclusion:

Many of the things that were seen as self-evident about the marital regime in which most Americans operated for 150 years are no longer self-evident. What seems in retrospect like the natural evolution of an institution probably did not feel that way at the time. The institutions that really stay with us, like the Constitution of the United States, do so only because they change. Keeping something in a rigid form does not prove to be the best way to make it last. The institution of marriage has absorbed many changes and proved extremely resilient, which shows that it is something people do want to continue to honor and keep. To say that it would be too great a shock to the institution, to go beyond the restriction of marriage to heterosexual couples, is probably an exaggeration; it would be a great change, but it might be just another form of adaptation. In every way except the difference of sex, marriages of same-sex couples reiterate the traditional values of monogamy. It may be that this change—the extension of marriage to same-sex couples—is actually positive for the continuation of the marriage institution.[28]

Both Nancy Cott and George Chauncey have made it their passion to portray the past in a way that impacts America's future, shaping it into conformance with their twisted beliefs about sex and gender. There are two primary reasons history can be taught from their perspective with immunity. One is that of "academic freedom," as Chauncey describes in his July 1998 *Chronicle of Higher Education* article entitled "The Ridicule of Gay and Lesbian Studies Threatens All Academic Inquiry."[29]

I know that this has been a lot to wade through. But ask yourself this question: How would your children survive a steady diet of such instruction if you find it so difficult just to read a brief description of what is going on in America's colleges and universities?

By the way, do you have any doubt why far more college graduates support homosexual rights than do those who have never attended college? There are very few people who can withstand this kind of constant pounding and not be moved in the direction of these dominant voices of academia.

Wishing for a Million Mogadishus

In April 2003, the *Chronicle of Higher Education* reported, "During a teach-in last month at Columbia, Mr. De Genova, a 35-year-old assistant professor of anthropology and Latino studies, told 3,000 students and faculty members that he hoped Iraq would defeat the United States. He also wished for 'a million Mogadishus,' a reference to the 1993 battle in Somalia in which 18 U.S. soldiers were killed."[30] Furthermore, De Genova admits that he "did trace a historical relationship between U.S. invasions and conquests and colonization to the history of white supremacy and racism in the U.S."[31] His comments were insulting enough to compel 104 members of Congress to send a letter to Columbia demanding that he be fired. University president Lee Bollinger may have tried to distance himself from De Genova's "outrageous comments" for PR purposes, but

Professor De Genova was still in his office well over a year after the incident.[32]

It probably comes as no surprise that universities are hotbeds of antiwar activity. The extent of this activity, however, is hard to overestimate. Historians have been leading the charge against President Bush's decision to remove the regime of Saddam Hussein from Iraq.

We do not see an atmosphere of cautious and scholarly critique. De Genova's outrageous cries for the death of American soldiers may be the most outlandish, but he has competition. Glenda Gilmore, who teaches at Yale, claimed that the reason President Bush ordered the invasion of Iraq is because he "wanted to be the emperor of the world."[33] She also claimed that he was "all hat and no brain."[34] One could reasonably question whether her wild claims about Bush's motives would justify applying the "all hat and no brain" appellation to her—that is, if she owns a hat.

At a meeting of the American Historical Association in January 2003, attendees formed an organization called Historians Against the War (HAW) and began collecting signatures for the statement below:

> We historians call for a halt to the march towards war against Iraq. We are deeply concerned about the needless destruction of human life, the undermining of constitutional government in the U.S., the egregious curtailment of civil liberties and human rights at home and abroad, and the obstruction of world peace for the indefinite future.[35]

Only three months later, 2,209 faculty members at America's colleges and universities had signed their names. Universities with the most prestigious history departments in the country boasted numbers comparable to the thirty-nine listed from Columbia, thirty-six from the University of Chicago, eighteen from Stanford, and sixteen from Yale.

A new statement was drafted by HAW in September 2003, with the title "Statement on the U.S. Occupation of Iraq." It quickly garnered over thirteen hundred signatures of its own. The revised pledge begins, "As historians, teachers, and scholars, we oppose the expansion of United States empire. . . . We deplore the secrecy, deception, and distortion of history involved in the administration's conduct of a war that violates international law, intensifies attacks on civil liberties, and reaches toward domination of the Middle East and its resources."[36]

With its extensive nationwide network of like-minded professors, HAW has lacked neither people nor enthusiasm as it organized rallies and teach-ins from California on the campus of Stanford University to New York during the 2004 Republican National Convention. HAW posts the thoughts of faculty members who want to share what they have done to promote worldwide peace. Anne Winkler-Morey of the University of Minnesota assures HAW colleagues that she "will be participating by talking about Iraq in [her] classes."[37] She also mentions that she is affiliated with Educators for Peace and Women Against Military Madness (a feminist organization that exists to "dismantle systems of militarism and global oppression").[38] Gilberto Reyes Jr., a history instructor at South Texas Community College, offered HAW a *McAllen Monitor* opinion editorial in which he argues, "Hispanics have a special responsibility to try to stop any war against any Muslim nation because we have more in common with Muslims than with most any other religious or ethnic group in the country."[39] The article concludes, "I hope U.S. Hispanics will unite to stop the war. To use an old Spanish word, ojalá (may Allah will it)."[40] HAW agreed, posting Reyes's example of activism in its "Virtual Movement Archive."

HAW has not forgotten Nicholas De Genova, the professor who called for "a million Mogadishus." Are they embarrassed by the extreme nature of his statements—such as wishing that brave, young Americans would be slaughtered and dragged through the streets? Hardly. Take a look at a Dear Colleague letter on the HAW Web site which reads:

> We write to ask you to join us in expressing concern over the public and university backlash against Professor Nicholas De Genova by attaching your name and institutional affiliation to the letter below. . . .
>
> At a time when all of our rights to free speech, non-violent association, and legal dissent are under attack, we support Professor De Genova's right to have spoken freely as an invited participant to an open forum. We would like to register our strong opposition to any personal, professional, or legal, retaliation that might be directed at him for having made these remarks.[41]

Organized history professors believe in defending their right of freedom of speech but criticize a president who believes in defending the nation that has done more to protect that freedom than any other civilization in human history. If they were professors of mathematics, their lack of any meaningful understanding of the lessons of history would be slightly less ironic.

On the Home Front

If you opened up the *New York Times* on March 27, 2000, you would have been confronted by the large-print announcement, "Charlton Heston Didn't Write the Second Amendment. He Just Acts That Way."[42] The ad continued, "Today NRA president Charlton Heston received a letter, signed by many of our nation's most prominent historians and legal scholars, urging the NRA to end its misrepresentation of the Second Amendment."[43] Misrepresentation, in their opinion, according to signer and professor Carl T. Bogus, means construing the Second Amendment as a defense of a "dual right" that consists of both the individual right to bear arms for self-defense and the collective right to maintain a government-regulated militia.[44] The letter to Heston concluded, "The central issue on which we all should focus is what sort of firearms legislation and policies will best prevent the killings and violence that plague our country today."[45]

Historians such as these suddenly present themselves as the defenders of constitutional orthodoxy. Jack Rakove is an esteemed, Harvard-educated professor of political science, history, and American studies at Stanford University. He has also taken a keen interest in constitutional interpretation. His books include *Original Meanings: Politics and Ideas in the Making of the Constitution and Interpreting the Constitution: The Debate Over Original Intent*. In regard to the Second Amendment, he says, "If you look at what was debated in 1787 and 1788, the main issue was the status of the militia, not individual rights."[46] This apparently provides enough proof for him to conclude that "the law comes down on the side of regulatory power in the interests of public health and safety."[47]

At first glance we might be tempted to applaud his apparent effort to maintain fidelity to the constitutional text, however erroneous his conclusions may be. If we look closer at his theory of interpretation, though, we discover that he is far from faithful. Here is what he wrote in his Pulitzer Prize-winning book *Original Meanings*:

> I am often asked whether I think originalism offers a viable or valid theory of constitutional interpretation. My preferred answer is, I hope, suitably ambivalent. In the abstract, I think that originalism is vulnerable to two powerful criticisms. First, it is always in some fundamental sense antidemocratic, in that it seeks to subordinate the judgment of present generations to the wisdom of their distant (political) ancestors. Second, the real problems of reconstructing coherent intentions and understandings from the evidence of history raise serious questions about the capacity of originalist forays to yield the definitive conclusions that the advocates of this theory claim to find. On the other hand, I happen to like originalist arguments when the weight of the evidence seems to support the constitutional outcomes I favor—and that may be as good a clue to the appeal of originalism as any other.[48]

The truth comes out. He "happen[s] to like originalist arguments when the weight of the evidence seems to support the constitutional outcomes [he] favor[s]." Though Rakove postures as a neutral scholar with claimed ambivalence, in reality he is simply disingenuous. He uses a methodology only when he believes it serves his political agenda. And he dares to attack Charlton Heston for misrepresentation?

The irony does not end there. Rakove joined four hundred other historians under the banner of "Historians in Defense of the Constitution" who contributed funds to run a full-page ad in the *New York Times* on October 30, 1998. Fifty-one were professors at the Ivies. What caused their distress? They were protesting the impending impeachment of then-President, William Jefferson Clinton. The November 3 edition of the *Stanford Daily* reported:

> The advertisement contained a six-paragraph statement, which opened "we deplore the present drive to impeach the President," stating that an impeachment would "have the most serious implications for our constitutional order."

> Calling the theory behind the current impeachment efforts "unprecedented," the historians asserted, "The new processes are extremely ominous for the future of our political institutions. If carried forward, they will leave the Presidency permanently disfigured and diminished, at the mercy as never before of the caprices of any Congress."[49]

Rakove fulfilled his part by taking a trip to Washington, D.C., to testify on behalf of Clinton at the House of Representatives' Constitution Committee hearing on the topic.

He and his colleagues across the nation justified their bold steps of action by explaining, "When you know something about the background of an issue, you have an obligation to try to explain it in the most intelligent and articulate way you can."[50] In the same article Rakove spilled the beans when he explained to the reporter that the advertisement was also partially funded by none other than the far-left political advocacy group, People for the American Way.[51]

Even beyond the taint of such funding, we have good reason to question Rakove's "scholarly" and "historical" defense of Clinton. It must be remembered that the whole idea of original intent constitutional analysis is to use history to help us find the correct meaning of our founding document. Rakove openly says that he favors the use of this methodology only when it favors the outcomes he desires. It is more than fair to conclude that Rakove's defense of Clinton was driven by his current political views—not his authentic views of the history of the Constitution.

Attacks on God and the Founding Fathers

Senior writer for *U.S. News and World Report* Michael Barone describes a disturbing phenomenon in his article "Forgetting the Founding Fathers." He notes that interest in America's founding has waned to such an extent that Lance Banning of the University of Kentucky was forced to conclude,

> Academics in general are as captivated by fads and fashions as any group I can think of, and the political, intellectual, diplomatic and military history of the Revolution and the Founding are decidedly out of fashion at the moment. Many history departments have little interest in hiring anyone who specializes in these sorts of interests, and a good many teachers of graduate students may well discourage such interests because they do not seem as attractive to hiring departments as studies in race, gender, identity and the like.[52]

Barone says that this priority on "race, class, and gender" has left only a remnant of elite university scholars who are pursuing research on colonial and revolutionary history.

He mentions Yale's Jon Butler as a member of this precious few. Could it be that there is a conservative historian at Yale specializing in early American studies? Not exactly. Well, to be more precise, not at all. Butler's status as a historical dinosaur comes not from his embrace of conservative principles, but from his failure to move on to the new, hip topics of gender and sexuality. His work has placed special emphasis on challenging any assertion that Christianity played any meaningful role in the founding of the American nation. Let's look at him more closely.

Jon Butler is a professor of American Studies, history, and religion. Before becoming the dean of the Yale's Graduate School of Arts and Sciences, he served as the chair of the Department of History. He is a prolific author and richly funded, prestigious researcher with a definitive voice on matters of American history. The U.S. Department of the Interior's National Park Service published one of his articles on its Web site entitled "American Revolution: Lighting Freedom's Flame." It describes the relationship between religion and the American Revolution with these sentences:

Religion was not a major cause of the American Revolution. . . .

Historians once emphasized that religious revivals during the so-called "Great Awakening" of the 1740s helped usher in the Revolution . . . [but] Revolutionaries themselves never used the revivals of the 1740s as models for Revolutionary protest in the 1760s and later.

Religious issues figured only occasionally in the protests leading to Revolution.[53]

This emphasis is typical of Butler's works. He takes advantage of every opportunity to "prove" that America's liberty, religious or otherwise, was the result of decidedly secular convictions.

For example, Butler cites Virginia's 1776 Declaration of Rights as evidence that Christianity was not a dominant force in early America because it "outlawed government aid to religion generally and protected freedom of worship for all religious groups in the state, not just for Christians."[54] Somehow he turned a blind eye to the last section of the Virginia Declaration, which states:

That religion, or the duty which we owe to our Creator, and the manner of discharging it, can be directed only by reason and conviction, not by force or violence; and therefore all men are equally entitled to the free exercise of religion, according to the dictates of conscience; and that it is the mutual duty of all to practise Christian forbearance, love, and charity toward each other.

Moreover, Butler fails to mention the fact that the chief support for these provisions in the Virginia Constitution came from Baptist ministers and other religious dissenters who had suffered under the hand of the established Anglican Church in Virginia.[55] It is simply bad history to suggest that the battle for religious liberty was won by secular forces. The blood of William Tyndale and the ashes of John Wycliff, both of whom were true scholars, cries out in protest against such superficial, antihistorical analysis.

Butler's essay "Why Revolutionary America Wasn't a 'Christian' Nation" explains that during the years prior to and following the American Revolution, Christianity was far from the culture-shaping influence that many observe. Instead, we read that occultism and magic, "traditional African religious expression," and Native American practices

78

shaped Christianity through a process of syncretism.[56] Butler is particularly adamant in pointing out that Puritanism and the Great Awakening had negligible effects on colonial society.

Is this true? The Library of Congress's exhibition entitled "Faith of Our Fathers: Religion and the Founding of the American Republic" answers in the negative. From the "passionately held religious convictions" of the earliest settlers to the "religion section" of George Washington's farewell address, Christian ideals, principles, and assurances were intertwined with life and culture.[57] According to this display of documents and artifacts at the Library of Congress, "there can be no doubt that religion played a major role in the Revolution by offering, through the sermons, pamphlets and actions of the American clergy, a moral sanction for opposition to the British, an assurance to the average American that opposition to the mother country was justified in the sight of God."[58]

Butler's assertions to the contrary are not innocuous. His thoughts count for something in modern America, as a quick glance at his *curriculum vitae* reveals.[59] In January 2004, PBS aired a discussion between media guru Bryant Gumbel, Heritage Foundation's Joseph Loconte, and Jon Butler on their evaluation of whether "under God" belongs in the Pledge of Allegiance. The context was the U.S. Supreme Court case, *Elk Grove United School District v. Newdow*. When asked whether the Founding Fathers would have considered "the notion of God so relevant in American life" that he merited mention in the Pledge, Butler answered, "Those who were very active in the ratification of the Constitution would, in fact, have said, 'No we shouldn't have this [under God].'"[60] The *Yale Herald* published a similar interview a few months later, but Butler's side was the only one presented.[61] Butler may wish to dust off his copy of the Constitution. It concludes with the notation that it was written in "the year of our Lord 1787." If references to God are in violation of the Constitution, why is there one in the very text of the document?

John Demos is another Yale history professor. He was educated at Harvard and UC Berkeley and is a Bancroft Prize-winning author. One of his classes for the 2004–2005 term is "Identities: Aspects of American and European Social and Cultural History," which "addresses the historical literature surrounding problems of identities, defined in a host of ways—racial, gendered, ethnic, regional, national, psychological, and age-related."[62] It appears that he is not a part of Barone's remnant, even though he does specialize in early American history.

Although Demos may be a superb historian in some respects, he is questionable in others. The June 2002 issue of the *Journal of American History* includes his essay, "Using Self, Using History . . ." Here, he chronicles how he moved from the pursuit of "objectivity" in his historical research to the incorporation of his "sense of self" into his scholarly activities. Demos begins his justification by describing the "small but vociferous cadre of New Left scholars" with which he grew to identify.[63] He explains that they planted the idea in his mind that a scholar could—or maybe should—be an activist as well. As Demos's thinking changed, he began to incorporate what he learned from Freud's theories of psychoanalysis into his studies on early American family life, witchcraft history, and Native American kidnappings and massacres. He purposely picks topics that focus on the "dark side" of American history because he feels that the patriotism instilled in him by parents, teachers, and mentors was misleading.[64] "Not only did he use himself and his experience for the sake of his projects," the *Journal* abstract announces, "the projects, for their part, were using him."[65]

There would be less concern if all Demos did was amuse himself with such activities. Yet, as a professor at Yale, he shapes the minds of the next generation. The clear implication is that he teaches the dark side of America so that old-fashioned patriotism will no longer be instilled in the future leaders of this nation.

Historical Illiteracy

Given the interpretations of American history outlined above, perhaps we should be grateful that most of America's elite institutions of higher education do not require students to study it. The American Council of Trustees and Alumni published a report in September 2002, conducted by the ACTA's Defense of Civilization Fund and the Center for Survey Research and Analysis at the University of Connecticut. It concluded that graduates of America's colleges and universities possess an "alarming ignorance of their heritage and a profound historical illiteracy."[66]

Could they be exaggerating? Here are some of the results of a Roper survey issued to seniors at the top twenty-five national universities and top twenty-five national liberal arts colleges, as defined by *U.S. News and World Report*:

- Only 23 percent could identify Madison as the "Father of the Constitution."
- Only 22 percent answered correctly that the phrase "government of the people, by the people, and for the people" is from the Gettysburg Address.

- Only 60 percent could identify the correct half century in which the American Civil War took place.

By contrast, 98 percent of the same seniors knew that Snoop Doggy Dogg is a rap singer, and 99 percent recognized Beavis and Butthead as television cartoon characters.

To emphasize the point, Appendix C in the report documents the history and social science requirements of the same fifty schools. Only 10 percent require students to take any kind of history course, generously defined. Not one college or university (of these 50) requires a course in American history as a prerequisite for graduation! Of the schools that do require general history, students are offered "The Cuban Revolution: 1956–1971: A Self Debate" as one choice, as at Harvard, or some class that fulfills a World Cultures requirement ("designed to help the student 'recognize cultures that have shaped and continue to shape the human experience and analyze materials that provide clues as to how these cultures work'"), as at Carnegie Mellon University.

Pulitzer Prize-winning author and historian David McCullough has taken a special interest in raising awareness about America's historical illiteracy. In a National Book Awards acceptance speech, after noting reports revealing that the "decided majority" of high school seniors are clueless about history, McCullough said:

> But I speak also from experience. On a winter morning on the campus of one of our finest colleges, in a lively Ivy League setting with the snow falling outside the window, I sat with a seminar of some twenty-five students, all seniors majoring in history, all honors students—the cream of the crop. "How many of you know who George Marshall was?" I asked. None. Not one.

At a large university in the Midwest, a young
woman told me how glad she was to have attended
my lecture, because until then, she explained, she
had never realized that the original thirteen
colonies were all on the eastern seaboard.[67]

The U.S. Congress also recognizes the implications of
this tragic reality. A concurrent resolution that passed unan-
imously in both Senate and House of Representatives during
the summer of 2000 cited the ACTA/Roper study. The document resolves:

Whereas America's colleges and universities are
leading bellwethers of national priorities and values, setting standards for the whole of the United
States' education system and sending signals to
students, teachers, parents, and public schools
about what every educated citizen must know . . .

Whereas the distinguished historians and intellectuals fear that without a common civic memory
and a common understanding of the remarkable individuals, events, and ideals that have shaped the
Nation, people in the United States risk losing
much of what it means to be an American, as well
as the ability to fulfill the fundamental responsibili-
ties of citizens in a democracy . . .

Now, therefore, be it Resolved by the Senate
(the House of Representatives concurring), That it
is the sense of Congress that . . . the historical illiteracy of America's college university graduates is a
serious problem that should be addressed by the
Nation's higher education community [and, inter
alia] parents should encourage their children to

select institutions of higher education with substantial history requirements.[68]

Clearly, these legislators recognize that unless America's young citizens understand their nation's past, they will be unable to govern either themselves or the country when the time comes.

Our history and the ideals that formed us as a people are what give us identity as Americans rather than our ethnic background or the color of our skin. What will happen when this identity is lost and the "diversities" of race, class, and gender take its place?

America's next generation needs an accurate understanding of our history in order to lead the nation correctly. Colleges and universities today are not doing their job. Increasingly, the goal of a liberal education is becoming so narrow that there is no such thing as a unified, "common body of knowledge" that seeks to transcend the narrow perspectives of individual disciplines. In colleges' quest to have it all, they seem to have lost everything that was worth keeping. They no longer bother themselves with forming the mind, character, and skills of "the human being the student is becoming."[69]

The solution to these problems cannot take the form of requiring more history classes at the typical elite universities. We need a different approach to history that is both accurate and not ashamed to instill old-fashioned notions like patriotism, virtue, and fidelity into the hearts of students.

CHAPTER 5

From John Adams to Alan Dershowitz: The Devolution of Legal Education

Of the fifty-six signers of the Declaration of Independence, twenty-five were trained as lawyers or jurists.[1] An even greater percentage of the delegates to the Constitutional Convention were lawyers: thirty-five of fifty-five were trained or practicing attorneys.[2]

Despite widespread anti-lawyer humor (much of which is justified and quite funny), Americans still select lawyers as a disproportionately high percentage of their political leaders. In 2003, approximately half of the governors, more than half of the United States Senate, and more than a third of the members of the House of Representatives were lawyers.[3]

In some respects it makes a lot of sense to have lawyers as political leaders. After all, the purpose of Congress is to enact, and hopefully repeal, provisions of the law. People trained in reading and understanding law have a natural advantage in such matters.

When we think of the phrase "professional training," we envision a fairly neutral course of study where doctors are trained in the details of anatomy or how to perform a certain surgical technique. Accountants can be taught to manage a chart of accounts. Bankers are taught the protocols for preparing loan documents and the calculation of declining interest rates. But in each of these fields, there is also a philosophical component. The philosophical component of a law school education is at least as great, if not greater than, any other form of professional education. And it is decidedly left-wing on the whole.

This leftward tilt can be seen on the macro level. Every law school that is a member of the American Association of Law Schools—and the 166 top law schools in the country are all members—is required to prohibit discrimination on campus against homosexuals. They also will not allow law firms that do not sign a similar nondiscrimination pledge to recruit on campus. The legal education industry has forthrightly come down on one side of the political debate over homosexual rights. Take a wild guess where our politics on this subject came from and where it is headed.

Duncan Kennedy, who has been teaching at Harvard Law School since the 1970s, is open about his desire to use law school to turn students into leftist political activists. In an article entitled "First Year Law Teaching as Political Action," Kennedy writes that he is "trying to transform the first-year experience into an intense form of political education."[4] Here are some of the specifics:

I propose that we develop our first year courses into systematic embodiments of our views about the present and future organization of social life. In particular, we should teach our students that bourgeois or liberal legal thought is a form of mystification. We should teach our students to understand the contradictions of that thought, and we should make utopian proposals to them about how to overcome those contradictions. . . .

Indeed, my politics consists entirely of four points: (1) a partial but dogmatic critique of liberal, bourgeois theories of law, economy and society; (2) a large measure of consistent and unpleasant revulsion at the way things work and the role I play in the working of things; (3) utopian fragments, very egalitarian, somewhat erotic and aesthetic, but imprecise even as fragments; and (4) a measure of steadily flowing hope about particular moments of political practice, situations of breakthrough when the encrustations of the [expletive deleted] hierarchy dissolve. . . .

We believe in a critique of liberal, bourgeois legalism that has considerable systematic quality. That critique can be summed up as follows: (1) no legal rule has to be what it is; (2) the ensemble of legal rules constitutes our capitalism; and (3) our capitalism is awful. Even if my utopian notions are too diffuse to teach, this triad of propositions is not.[5]

Columbia University's Robert Ferguson says that "as a law professor," he wants to "show students how the past influences the present."[6] Ferguson maintains, "Only if they know the history of law are they ready to reform the law. I want to train lawyers who think about changing and reforming the law."[7]

Janet Halley also teaches at Harvard. In an interview on a book she wrote that decries rules against open homosexuality in the military, she made clear how she wants her students to think and act after taking her courses. She stated, "The book functions in a lot of dimensions. It's a law-reform piece, but it's also a piece of high queer theory, and it's also law and humanities work of the kind that I'm trying to encourage students to do."[8]

Making Laws . . .

Laws are the official rules of a formal society. There is a philosophy that underlies any set of rules, and American law is no exception. The philosophy of legal education today will necessarily have a dominant impact on the laws created by our federal, state, and local governments in the years ahead. A considerable number of our elected officials are not only members of the legal profession themselves—virtually all have staff attorneys to guide their decisions.

For Bible-believing Christians and others who respect the philosophy of the American founding, there is a considerable basis for concern, if not alarm, about the future of our Republic based on the nature of elite legal education in America at the dawn of the twenty-first century.

The problems we find in American legal education can be summarized in three basic areas:

- Original intent of the Constitution is rejected in favor of an evolving interpretation.
- The principle of the rule of law is tortured into a rule of arbitrary governance.
- God's moral law is utterly rejected as having any legitimate role in American law.

Before I launch into a detailed description of each of these problems, it is helpful to review some of the basic principles upon which our Constitution and legal system were founded. The most basic principle of our Constitution is not found in the First Amendment. Unsurprisingly, it is found in Article I, Section 1, which states, "All legislative powers herein granted shall be vested in a Congress of the United States, which shall consist of a Senate and House of Representatives."

Why does this section contain the most basic principle? We need to remember the fundamental reason for the American Revolution. Great Britain passed laws that imposed taxes and otherwise asserted its authority over the American colonies in ways that denied the long-standing right of self-government. To be sure, our colonial legislatures were under the authority of the crown, but that was true of the British Parliament as well. Laws passed by a colonial legislature were subject to approval or disapproval by the Crown (or its representative), and there was no process to override a royal veto. But the central contention of our forefathers was that no law could be made without the consent of our own elected representatives.

We lose some of the important nuances of the thinking of our political ancestors when we focus superficially on the phrase, "No taxation without representation." The American Revolution was not a protest over the rate of taxation but over the authority of the British Parliament to impose any law whatsoever.

These lessons were not forgotten when the Constitutional Convention convened in 1787. The question, "Who has the authority to make law?" was still the fundamental issue. The convention was split over the question of the composition of the legislative branch. But there was never any doubt that all lawmaking authority would be given to legislators who directly (the House) or indirectly (the Senate) represented the people.

There was never any suggestion that the President would be allowed to make law. Those who campaigned against the ratification of the Constitution were quick to find parallels between the King of England and the proposed powers of the presidency. If there had been a shadow of lawmaking authority intended—a power which even the king did not possess—the hue and cry of "Despotism!" would have been significantly greater and, without any doubt, the Constitution would not have been ratified.

Just as the President was never intended to have the authority to make law, the Constitution never intended to give the judiciary any lawmaking authority whatsoever. One easy way to prove this point is to look at the common law. Common law is made by judges and many states allow their judges to continue this practice. However, it is undisputed that federal judges have no common law authority. Since there is no federal common law.

Christians today are often enamored with the common law. But, frankly, we confuse the content of the common law with the process by which it was obtained.

What we tend to like in the common law is the obvious parallel between much of the common law and biblical morality. Consider one rule of the common law for a moment, though, and see how much you like it.

Under the common law, if you were injured in an accident where you were 1-percent negligent and Jones, the other person in the accident, was 99-percent negligent, you could receive nothing at all in a lawsuit to recover your damages. This is the common law rule of contributory negligence. If you contribute at all to your own harm, you get nothing. (This rule has been changed in America mostly in the last thirty years or so.) Now, how much do you like that aspect of common law?

The significant feature of the common law was not its content but the process by which it was made. Judges over time "discerned" the common rules that were followed by decent society. So long as the society overwhelmingly has a Christian worldview, common rules will be generally good. But it would be better to realize that what we really like is the natural law—that is, God's law which can be discovered, first and foremost, in the Bible. To some lesser extent, it can also be discovered in the general rules written on the hearts of every man. The common law is mainly a process. Natural law is all about substance.

The process of the making of the common law is made is actually antithetical to the principles of the American founding. Our elected legislators are to make the law, not unelected judges who can change the law at their whim over time.

Accordingly, the federal courts were not given common law power, and there was a clear, albeit implicit, decision to deny to the federal judiciary the power to make law in any field including constitutional law.

The American founders wanted a republic, not a judicially controlled oligarchy.

How do these philosophical principles fare in today's law schools? Not very well, as you are about to see.

The Rejection of Original Intent

In the field of law nothing is more fundamental than one's view of the Constitution of the United States. Our founders wanted the Constitution (and ultimately the Bill of Rights) to be viewed, in the words of James Madison, as "fundamental maxims of free Government" that would be "a good ground for an appeal to the sense of community" against potential oppression and would "counteract the impulses of interest and passion."[9] The Constitution was to be the people's document by which they would hold their officials accountable.

Any appropriate theory of constitutional interpretation will take this idea into account. The provisions of the Constitution need to be understandable by average people. The rules of interpretation need to be simple and clear, not complex or convoluted.

Let's jump with both feet into the midst of modern legal education's view of constitutional interpretation. Is it simple and clear? Michael Dorf, professor of law at Columbia University, wrote an article published in the *California Law Review* (University of California at Berkeley) entitled "Create Your Own Constitutional Theory." Here's the description of his approach:

> Critics of constitutional pragmatism, such as Professor Fallon, argue that courts should not decide constitutional cases simply by asking what outcome is best, all things considered. Such an approach, the critics contend, does not permit constitutional adjudication to advance values associated with democracy, the rule of law, and individual rights. This Reply to Professor Fallon's article in this issue argues that the critics are right to reject pure adjudicatory instrumentalism, but that a different conception of pragmatism should inform constitutional interpretation. Early twentieth-century American philosophers used the term *pragmatism* to mean understanding a practice by participating in it rather than theorizing about it. Applied to constitutional law, this notion of pragmatism-as-contextualism

makes instrumentalism safe for interpretation, for it allows instrumental considerations to be weighed within the felt-but-difficult-to-define constraints imposed by constitutional practice. In endorsing constitutional pragmatism-as-contextualism, this Reply challenges Professor Fallon's suggestion that judges and constitutional scholars should "choose" constitutional theories that they then use to resolve concrete disputes. Instead, this Reply argues that theories of constitutional interpretation emerge from considered, contextual judgments about particular cases.[10]

Don't worry if you had a hard time reading this description of Dorf's theories that appeared as an official introduction to his full argument. Can anyone claim that even James Madison would find this academic gibberish as "easy to understand?"

What Dorf argues (and it took me several reads to brush away his verbal fog) is that interpretation of the Constitution should "emerge" from deciding cases by what judges think is right independent of any consideration of the text of the document. After several cases are decided in a particular area, then you have a doctrine of constitutional law. Decide what you want. Then change the meaning of the Constitution to match what you wanted to decide in the first place. (Unfortunately, Dorf is exactly correct when he says that his theory basically sums up how constitutional law actually functions in most cases.)

When Dorf's principles are declared with verbal eloquence, they have a captivating force upon a student who, in general, desperately desires to be perceived as being among the superintelligent. Someone who can write with such complex eloquence must be brilliant. And if he is brilliant, then the substance of his ideas must be worthy of consideration or adoption.

But if you state Dorf's principles in plain language, anyone can see that he is proposing nothing more than a shell game. Decide what you want. And then announce that the decision was dictated by a binding principle of constitutional law.

It is fair to wonder if Dorf is a renegade. Are his views the common, prevailing view? Certainly not in the details. It seems that nearly every professor of constitutional law at a major school has his or her own pet theory of interpretation that may differ from Dorf's "constitutional pragmatism-as-contextualism." But the differences are only in the details. The dominant majority categorically reject the only true alternative—originalism. After all, following the intentions of the founding fathers is far too simplistic. It fails to appeal to their inner need to appear to be brilliant.

Dorf was responding to Professor Fallon, another professor from Harvard. Does Fallon argue for original intent? You decide:

> Upon close examination, judicial legitimacy does not turn on consent to be governed by the written Constitution (and it alone), as is often thought, but on contemporary acceptance and the reasonable justice of the prevailing regime of law. In light of longstanding acceptance and considerations of justice and prudence, *stare decisis* deserves recognition as a legitimate, constitutionally authorized doctrine beyond Congress's power to control. . . .
>
> However much we might wish for some more solid rock of support, our entire constitutional order rests on the potentially shifting sands of acceptance and reasonable justice.[11]

Fallon argues that when the Supreme Court has created a precedent that it refuses to change over a long period, then this "rule of law" effectively becomes a part of the Constitution. Even a faint resemblance to originalism is not to be found in this theory. Instead, it is an utter rejection of republicanism, the theory that only our elected legislators can make our laws.

Morton Horwitz, also a professor at Harvard, notes that progressives (that is, socialist liberals) were enamored with the idea of original intent at one point but ultimately have come to realize that it is a tool of conservatives like former Reagan Attorney General Ed Meese. He writes:

So, originalism, which originally had progressive possibilities, has totally been preempted by the Meesean argument. Despite the intellectual difficulties of originalism, which we spent twenty years reciting upside down and inside out, originalism institutionalizes a conservative effort to take a static snapshot of 1789 that freezes the Federalist hostility to democracy. So though we can make lots of headway out of originalism in particular cases, it does seem to be, as Attorney General Meese so well understood, stacked in favor of conservative constructs.[12]

Yet another professor at Harvard Law School has taken direct aim at original intent as a method of constitutional interpretation. Like many of his academic colleagues, Frank Michelman wrote in disgust after the Supreme Court denied the homosexual demand for a new constitutional right in the *Bowers* case in the 1980s. Michelman is clear. He hates both the theory of original intent and its results, as the following article excerpt reveals:

What ought chiefly to alarm liberals about the *Bowers* decision, then, is not a judicial affection for moral majoritarianism that the Justices collectively almost certainly do not hold and could not propagate if they did. Rather, it is the decision's embodiment of an excessively detached and passive judicial stance toward constitutional law. The devastating effect in *Bowers* of a judicial posture of deference to external authority appears in the majority's assumption, plain if not quite explicit in its opinion, that public values meriting enforcement as law are to be uncritically equated with either the formally enacted preferences of a recent legislative or past constitutional majority, or with the received teachings of an historically dominant, supposedly civic, orthodoxy. I will call such a looking backward jurisprudence authoritarian because it regards adjudicative actions as legitimate only insofar as dictated by the prior normative utterance, express or implied, of extra-judicial authority.[13]

Let's spend a little time unpacking what Michelman is saying. First, he is making fun of the idea that the *Bowers* decision was consistent with traditional ideas of morality. He utterly rejects the idea that the Supreme Court holds such moral principles in high esteem—and, alas, he is absolutely right about that. What bothers him most is summed up in his contention that the decision was an "excessively detached and passive judicial stance toward constitutional law." If the Supreme Court started following the original intent of the framers, this would interfere with the liberal use of the courts to achieve their political objectives on a whole range of issues.

Michelman notes that when original intent is followed, the only kinds of public policy decisions that can be enforced in courts are these:

- Formally enacted preferences of a recent legislative majority
- A past constitutional majority
- The received teachings of a historically dominant, supposedly civic, orthodoxy

In other words, the only sources of laws are statutes passed by legislatures, the text of the Constitution, and natural law. He hates the fact that these are the sole sources of law because it leaves out "adjudicative actions" as a legitimate source of law. In other words, he detests original intent because it does not allow the Supreme Court to make up law out of thin air.

No one should believe that Harvard is alone in this position. For one thing, a great number of professors at other schools got their law degrees at Harvard. Cass Sunstein at the University of Chicago is one example. He openly advocates what he calls a "common law method of constitutional law." This means that the judges should be allowed to change the Constitution over time, just like judges in England were able to change the laws of contracts or criminal law under their tradition of common law. He contends that "clear statement principles, agency interpretations, and democratic ideals [should] supplement and occasionally countermand the text as understood at the time of enactment."[14]

There it is, as clear as the Left knows how to say it. These other sources of law—that judges are allowed to choose as they alone see fit—are not only allowed to add to our Constitution's original intent, but they are also allowed to overrule the original meaning of the text.

You may have noted the phrase "democratic ideals" in Sunstein's litany of new sources of law. This is more than a little ironic. Democratic ideals are about self-government—only our elected legislature can make our laws. The Left has changed the meaning of democracy to achieve its ends. When they say they believe in promoting democracy, they have absolutely nothing in common with the work of Sam Adams, Patrick Henry, or James Madison.

What do these elite law schools teach as the meaning of democracy? What are these ideals that they urge their students to embrace as a method of interpreting the Constitution?

Our friend Morton Horwitz starts us off with his words, "In my view, it is not possible to argue that democracy was really in the original constitution."[15] If our Constitution is not democracy, then what is? Here's Horwitz's version: "Are democracy and progressive jurisprudence the same? Maybe they are not entirely the same but they are not that different."[16] He adds,

> Progressive Jurisprudence encourages us to think of law in terms of protecting the weak and the scorned as a means of encouraging distributive justice and, therefore, greater equality, because you cannot have democracy without relative equality of power and privilege that makes democratic culture possible.[17]

And, he says, we should "protect a wider notion of democratic culture as arguably First Amendment obscenity cases are all about."[18]

Let's sum up and translate into ordinary language. Democratic ideas are about distributive justice—taking money from the rich and powerful and giving to the poor and weak. In other words, they are socialist, at the least, or outright Marxist economic and political theories. The chief current example of what he means by "protecting the scorned" is the elimination of all legal distinctions between homosexuals and heterosexuals. It also means more openness—that is, more obscenity.

There you have it. The new definition of democracy. Socialism and moral libertarianism. Our Constitution should be interpreted to achieve these results as the new democratic ideals.

Rejection of the Rule of Law

The core meaning of "the rule of law" was noted by dissenting Justice Black, in the 1970 Supreme Court decision, *In Re Winship*:

> But the struggle [of the Founding Fathers] had not been simply to put all the constitutional law in one document, it was also to make certain that men would be governed by law, not the arbitrary fiat of the man or men in power.[19]

One essential application of this meaning is that all citizens—rulers and ordinary citizens alike—have an equal duty to obey the law. No man is above the law. Ironically, Richard Nixon gave one of the strongest statements of this meaning of the rule of law when he stated:

> Every judge, every attorney, every law enforcement official wants to "do justice." But the only way that can be accomplished, the only way justice can truly be done in any society, is for each member of that society to subject himself to the rule of law— neither to set himself above the law in the name of justice, nor to set himself outside the law in the

name of justice. We shall become a genuinely just
society only by "playing the game according to the
rules" and, when the rules become outdated or are
shown to be unfair, by lawfully and peaceably
changing those rules.[20]

The rule of law prohibits the tyrannical practice of un-
equal justice. A system which prefers one race, one religion,
or one's friends when dispensing justice violates a core
meaning of "the rule of law."

Likewise, Ronald Reagan said in 1983:

Thomas Jefferson said his criteria for honor and
status was not wealth, but virtue and talent. In
"Abraham Lincoln: The Prairie Years," Carl
Sandburg wrote that Lincoln believed "the accent
and stress was to be on opportunity, on equal
chance, equal access to the resources of life, liberty,
and the pursuit of happiness. To give man this
equal chance in life was the aim, the hope, the flair
of glory, spoken by the Declaration of
Independence."

Through the years, this promise was made real,
thanks to the hard work, the dedication, and commitment to freedom of the American people. Our
commitment to freedom has meant commitment to
the rule of law.[21]

The rule of law is a principal distinction between free
nations and totalitarian regimes. In the words of Harry S
Truman,

The economic plight in which Europe now finds
itself has intensified a political struggle between
those who wish to remain free men living under
the rule of law and those who would use economic

distress as a pretext for the establishment of a totalitarian state.[22]

The rule of law is an essential component of our commitment to individual rights.

President Dwight Eisenhower declared:

Freedom under law is like the air we breathe. People take it for granted and are unaware of it—until they are deprived of it. What does the rule of law mean to us in everyday life? Let me quote the eloquent words of Burke: "The poorest man may, in his cottage, bid defiance to all the forces of the Crown. It may be frail; its roof may shake; the wind may blow through it; the storms may enter; the rain may enter—but the King of England cannot enter; all his forces dare not cross the threshold of that ruined tenement!"[23]

The American Republic was founded, not to overturn the rule of law, but to demand its continued application.

Finally, Gerald Ford commented in 1975:

The American Revolution was unique in its devotion to the rule of law. We overthrew our rulers but cherished their rules. The Founding Fathers were dedicated to John Locke's dictum that "where there is no law, there is no freedom." One of them, James Madison, added his own corollary, "If men were angels, no government would be necessary."[24]

The rule of law is a transcendent American value that is widely embraced by all sides of the political spectrum—at least in their public rhetoric.

But what is being taught in elite law schools on this subject? Do they embrace the rule of law? Do they mean the same thing that was meant when our founding fathers used this term?

Mary Anne Case is a professor at the University of Chicago School of Law. Among other things, she spends her time conducting a "bathroom study" to bolster her argument that having gender-segregated restrooms is a bad idea. Unisex bathrooms would "give men and women less reason to separate in social functions."[25] (By the way, when I was helping Phyllis Schlafly and Beverly LaHaye defeat the Equal Rights Amendment, the Left always broke into riotous laughter when anyone mentioned the idea that their philosophy would lead to unisex bathrooms. Now a "serious" scholar at one of the top five law schools in the country is conducting her own survey to accomplish just such an objective.)

What does Professor Case teach about the rule of law when she actually has time to be in the classroom?

In a *University of Chicago Law Review* article attacking the Supreme Court's decision in *Bush v. Gore*, Case makes clear her contempt for the view that the law is a set of binding rules. She appealed to the Warren Court era of the 1970s, saying that the proper tradition was "the Constitution required rules to be relaxed into standards."[26] If the Supreme Court had relaxed the rules of the Constitution and converted them into "standards," then in *Bush v. Gore* they would have allowed the courts to review all of the ballots so that judges could make independent determinations of "the intent of the voter." Professor Case was outraged that the Court would choose rules over relaxed standards allowing the courts to do what they want.

She doesn't like "specific rules designed to ensure uniform treatment." She prefers "individualized determination." Good grief. What does she think the rule of law means?

The rule of law means uniformity of treatment for all so that justice will favor neither the rich nor the poor. But Professor Case is unhappy unless the rules are relaxed into standards so that judges can favor Democrats over Republicans.

She is not the only professor of "law" who decries the whole notion of law as a uniform and binding rule. David Strauss, also at the University of Chicago, wrote an article entitled "Must Like Cases Be Treated Alike?" If one actually believed in the rule of law, then the answer to this question would require only one word—"yes." Strauss disagrees. Like cases should not be treated alike if "identically situated people" . . . "live in different political communities or grew up in different families."[27] He continues, "In fact, a general requirement that like cases be treated alike can perpetuate injustice."

Once the Constitution itself is not a binding set of written rules, then the whole notion of the rule of law is effectively dead. When judges can make their own individualized determinations of what the text should mean, there is no such thing as a binding rule that our rulers cannot change at their whim. If this is the way the "highest law of the land" is treated, all other sources of law will receive no better treatment at the hands of a tyrannical judiciary.

When we lose the rule of law, we are no better than a corrupt, Third World country. A Hungarian journalist describes the desperate situation in that nation because of the failure of the rule of law as follows:

> The implementation of new rules pertaining
> to the punishment of minor offences has once
> again brought crime and its social costs to public

attention. The new fines are higher, and there is nothing to stop the police from pocketing the proceeds. And the lawyers are even more corrupt than the police. The rule of law might very well prevail on Hungary on paper, but in practice a quite different picture emerges—one of arbitrary arrest, of incompetence and indifference. We are not confronted here with a few rotten apples spoiling the contents of the barrel, but with a system which tolerates corruption, where bribery is an accepted oiling of the machinery, where an appropriate ethos of professional pride is entirely lacking.[28]

The American rule of law is not being perverted for petty economic reasons like in the former Soviet bloc nations. But it is still being perverted, and the ultimate results are no different. When judges are allowed to change the law at their whim and make individualized determinations to promote their own personal political philosophy, we have arbitrary government, not the rule of law.

And our future legal leaders are being taught that this is good.

Rejection of God's Moral Principles

I attended the oral argument in the Supreme Court case of *Lawrence v. Texas* in 2003. I knew that traditional values were in trouble when one of the justices asked the lawyer to give him a "straight answer" to a question. The audience and several members of the Court broke out into mocking laughter. Straight, gay. The elite hipness of the audience was evident. It was a dominantly pro-gay crowd.

The decision was not made because of audience pressure on the Supreme Court. Yet there is no doubt that the crowd had its effect. This is the social circle of the legal elite. The Supreme Court. The Ivy League professors. The top law students. The lawyers in the major firms who have come through this process. And they emotionally batter anyone who disagrees with their postmodern morality.

A few weeks after the Supreme Court decided the case of *Bowers v. Hardwick*, which upheld the traditional view of the law in this area and rejected any notion of a constitutional right to homosexuality, I ran into Justice White at Dulles Airport. Justice White wrote the majority opinion in *Bowers*.

I greeted Justice White and told him that I had written an amicus brief in *Bowers* and that I really appreciated his decision. He grumbled at me.

"You must be the only person in America who thinks so," he replied.

"No," I answered, "there are millions of people who support and appreciate your decision."

After a few more grumbling noises from the justice, his wife extended her hand to me in thanks. "I really appreciate your comments," she said.

It was obvious to me that Justice White had been getting the tar beaten out of him in his day-to-day social circles. It was wearing on him. His wife appreciated anyone who would speak an encouraging word.

Judges are human beings. When they run in a group that rejects the morality of God—in fact it mocks the morality of God—we must realize that plain old peer pressure is going to have an effect.

Harvard's Alan Dershowitz, who equates belief in God with belief in space aliens, openly castigates the most fundamental set of God's moral laws: "Not only do the Ten

Commandments not belong in public courthouses or classroom, they do not even belong—at least without some amendments and explanatory footnotes—in the hearts and minds of contemporary Americans."[29] And he teaches a course at Harvard on the scriptural sources of justice!

His Harvard colleague Frank Michelman blasts the *Bowers* decision because of the "justification of such a law [against sodomy] on the frightening ground that its specific moral motivation 'is firmly rooted in Judaeo-Christian moral and ethical standards.'"[30]

Peggy Cooper Davis from the New York University School of Law argues "that the United States constitutional system, as amended during Reconstruction, requires the tolerance generated by the moral independence view and forbids state action that has no purpose other than moral standard-setting."[31]

She wrote this in 1994. In 2003, the Supreme Court made her position the binding constitutional principle of our nation. The *Lawrence* decision did not only legitimize all homosexual conduct between consenting adults; it also ruled that no law may ever be passed that has the protection of morality as its sole purpose. At a minimum laws against pornography, prostitution, and drugs are in deep trouble because all of these are "victimless crimes" that seek to perpetuate a singular view of morality.

What is taught at elite law schools tends to find its way into Supreme Court decisions about ten years later.

No conservative plan to reform the judiciary will truly succeed until we develop robust alternatives to these top law schools.

CHAPTER 6

And That's the Way It Is: Journalism School Today— Media Bias Tomorrow

Late in the 2004 presidential race, Dan Rather made bold accusations against the President based on documents supposedly composed on a military typewriter in 1972. He saw nothing wrong with the fact that the documents were written in the Times Roman font—a font that was never used on a typewriter. He did not think it strange that numbers expressed like this—111th—are possible with computers but not common military typewriters from the 1970s. Rather was so anxious to harm the President that basic investigative protocols were ignored.

This was not factual reporting. This was political combat in the guise of news.

For forces on the Right, CBS veteran Bernard Goldberg aimed shots at the liberal media establishment when he wrote *Bias: A CBS Insider Exposes How the Media Distort the News*. On the Left, *The Nation* columnist Eric Alterman returned fire with his title, *What Liberal Media? The Truth about Bias and the News*.

Conservatives particularly relish digging up and publicizing examples of blatantly left-leaning headlines in major newspapers or comments made by Peter Jennings during the nightly news. While these instances ignite tempers and provide some hearty laughs, they also lend sober credence to studies that show, for instance, that media professionals are four times more likely to identify themselves as "liberal" rather than "conservative," not including "moderates."[1]

The central issue concerns more than politics. As former *World* publisher Joel Belz pointed out in an August 2004 article, "Whether the two sides in any debate are equally represented in the pages of a newspaper is hardly the point. Far more important is what the reporters and editors think about truth itself, about reality itself."[2] This brings us back to the idea of *worldview*. We have seen that philosophies that approach law, government, and history apart from the objective standards of God and his Word lead to twisted conclusions, and print journalism is no exception. The stakes are high. Terry Mattingly, a nationally syndicated religion columnist, says it this way:

There is no conspiracy to produce THE liberal media. You don't need a conspiracy when so many journalists go to the same schools, work their way up through the same media structures and respect the same cultural heroes, while hating the same enemies. . . . The divisions are real and they do affect the news, especially on cultural issues.[3]

Conspiracy or not, we can all fairly agree that biblical truth rarely appears on the pages of the *Washington Post*, the *New York Times*, and *USA Today*. If anything, "the Religious Right" is slighted or ridiculed. As Mattingly perceptively remarks, why should we puzzle over the media's left-leaning ideological tendencies when reporters, correspondents, and commentators receive, by and large, the same kind of training from America's colleges and universities?

Our focus in this chapter is primarily on print journalism. Other media of mass communication have their place, but the *written* word should be of particular concern to those of us who profess to believe that the sixty-six books of Scripture comprise God's inerrant revelation. Technology may change, but there will always be a place for solid, insightful writing.

Where They Come From

There is long-standing controversy in journalism circles. This debate has to do with the importance and emphasis of college education. While all agree that competence in subject matter (whether economics, law, health care, or legislative processes) is a necessity, some professionals say that the best way of learning how to be a journalist is simply to *be* one. Journalism school may be nice for some people, they say, but it can only go so far. In the words of Noel Greenwood, a long-time senior editor at the *Los Angeles Times*, "What you confront [when you become a journalist] is not this big continual problem of how to hang a paragraph—you confront the problem of social issues, historical issues, cultural issues, ethnic, government issues."[4] Earning a degree in one of those key substantive areas while writing up a storm for the university daily would give a prospective journalist a significant advantage.

There are variations among proponents of college education for journalists too. Some journalism schools maintain a trade-skill emphasis. The University of Missouri, for example, centers its curriculum on equipping students for the profession through classes on such things as professional ethics, news gathering, correspondence, and libel law. On the other hand, the journalism programs at Columbia University and the University of Wisconsin at Madison emerged during the early Progressive Era and are known for their focus on theoretical issues such as the "reform" role of the press in society. Columbia's journalism school was initiated by Joseph Pulitzer and reflected his mission of "improv[ing] society through improving journalism."[5]

As we now know, however, *no* education is just about facts, regardless of its purported emphasis. And given the prevailing philosophies at America's colleges and universities, it is only natural for journalism to reflect their course.

The reality today is that newsrooms are more likely than ever before to be filled with college grads. Often these graduates are from the most prestigious journalism schools. Columbia, Northwestern, the University of Missouri, and the University of Wisconsin at Madison are among the "Ivies," if you will, of the J-school world. John Leo, a *U.S. News and World Report* columnist, noted this phenomenon when he told a media bias panel, "It used to be that anybody could be a reporter by walking in the door. It's a little harder to do that now. . . . What you get is people from Ivy League colleges with upper-class credentials, what you get is people who more and more tend to be and act alike."[6]

The American Journalist is a highly regarded decennial report that aims to "measure the pulse" of the nation's journalists.[7] The 2002 study was conducted by the School of Journalism at Indiana University and sponsored by the John S. and James L. Knight Foundation. Among other things the findings indicate that nearly 90 percent of all journalists have a minimum of a four-year bachelor's degree.[8] Of that number half majored in communication or journalism.[9]

These numbers could be partially due to the increase in college graduates generally. It also, however, reflects the business nature of a newspaper. Noel Greenwood notes that newspaper management may find it much easier to keep a lid on spending by hiring a young person right out of Northwestern who can perform a variety of tasks, as opposed to hiring "a thirty-five-year-old medical writer who has been specializing in health coverage for the last ten years."[10]

Although this trend began with the advent of college journalism programs around the turn of the twentieth century, it did not truly take off until the post-World War II era. Press scholars Harry D. Marsh and David R. Davies inform us:

> College-educated reporters and editors came to
> dominate news rooms [from 1945–1974]. A
> mid–1950s study showed that fewer than 20% of
> the staff members of Texas papers had been to col-
> lege. An early 1970s study found that the figure
> was approaching 90%. College journalism courses
> burgeoned during the 1960s and 70s. Journalism
> courses dealt with historical, ethical, and theoreti-
> cal perspectives of the media, as well as with the
> practical skills needed to work for the media. Upon
> graduation students took their college perspectives
> to their jobs. They looked upon fellow students and
> their professors as professional partners, and they
> established informal nationwide networks of
> alumni and colleagues who shared their views.[11]

This passage states so clearly what we have already stressed repeatedly in this book: "Upon graduation students [take] their college perspectives to their jobs."

As educational institutions go, so, it seems, goes the nation. The stakes are perhaps higher in journalism than other fields because its capacity for influence extends across many fronts. What Americans know of Muslim extremists in Jakarta and nuclear experiments in North Korea, or of cloture votes in Congress or a class-action suit initiated by farmers in Kansas, arrives at living rooms and workplaces— more often than not—*through* the mainstream press. "Journalism," write Bill Kovach and Tom Rosenstiel, "provides something unique to a culture—independent, reliable, accurate, and comprehensive information that citizens require to be free. A journalism that is asked to provide something other than that subverts democratic culture."[12]

That sums it up well: journalism provides the information that citizens require to be free. Yet in today's America many journalists seem to specialize in undercutting the moral and religious forces that hold even more importance for our freedom. M. Stanton Evans, founder of the National Journalism Center in the Washington, D.C. area, describes the phenomenon as a "disconnect" between the big media and average citizens:

> The way we're taught history is also the way
> that most journalists look at our history because
> they're products of our educational system. And
> what that basically boils down to is a complete sec-
> ularism. Ideas that are pervasive in the academy
> also become pervasive in the media because that's
> where reporters come from. . . . That's where this
> gap begins. The big media are intensely secular; a

believing Christian or Jew in orthodox religious terms is very rare in the large media. Most of these folks are not believers in biblical religion—or, if they are, it's very sketchy, and there's not much understanding of it. And that generates a lot of hostility. . . . It's a religious matter.[13]

Evans comments further that whether the issue is abortion or homosexual marriage or the Ten Commandments in a county seal, reporters often see the activities of conservative Christians as "alien" or "strange" to them.

Given what we have learned about Columbia and company through the course of previous chapters, are graduates of these schools the kind of people that we want covering the issues that mean the most to us?

Objective Subjectivity?

Aren't journalists supposed to be objective? This used to be the ideal. The earliest journalism textbooks adopted "objectivity" as a "central tenet even before separate schools and departments of journalism were established."[14] For example, Robert Luce's *Writing for the Press: A Manual*, first published in 1886, instructed journalists:

"Never put an editorial opinion into a news paragraph," is a standard rule and, interpreted correctly, a good one. Theoretically it is not the province of the reporter or correspondent to express opinions. . . . Distinguish between your own opinions and the opinions of others: your own are insignificant; those of others, if they are men whose opinions carry weight, should often be reported, but so as to put the burden on them . . . let it appear as such and not as your own.[15]

Another book used by Washington College in one of America's first journalism courses was *Haney's Guide to Authorship* (1867), which said, "There should be no comments. The editor should not be a partizan [*sic*] of either side. He should chronicle the facts, but not give opinions."[16]

Journalists and the public they write for have become increasingly skeptical of the idea that news is "just facts," and "objectivity" has become hackneyed enough to merit elimination from the 1996 Society of Professional Journalists' Code of Ethics. As David Mindich notes in *Just the Facts: How "Objectivity" Came to Define American Journalism*, this growing "acknowledgement of human bias" is illustrated in the replacement of Walter Cronkite's concluding "And that's the way it is" with Dan Rather's "And that's part of *our* world" (emphasis added).[17]

Likewise, at Columbia University's School of Journalism, it seems that instruction has redefined the old-fashioned ideal of impartiality for something "better." What is the new ultimate value? Believe it or not, it is something akin to deliberate *sub*jectivity, although they would never call it that.

Brent Cunningham is the managing editor of the *Columbia Journalism Review*, a prestigious publication referred to as "the media's periodical of conscience."[18] He is also a Columbia faculty member. In the July/August 2003 issue of *CJR*, he wrote a thought-provoking cover article entitled "Re-thinking Objectivity." After opening with some tirades against President Bush's supposed rhetorical "spin" and tight-fistedness with information (especially related to national security matters), Cunningham announces a "particular failure of the press: allowing the principle of objectivity to make [them] passive recipients of news, rather than aggressive explainers of it."[19]

His disapproval of objectivity stems from his claims that it "exacerbates our tendency to rely on official sources," "excuses lazy reporting," "makes us wary of seeming to argue with the president," and "limits [the press's] ability to help set the agenda."[20] In the section of the article called "The Real Bias"—he says the most "damaging" kind of bias is socioeconomic—Cunningham describes the "reformist" mind-set that purportedly transcends the boundaries of political parties. In order to answer the charge of liberal bias, he quotes James Carey as saying, "There is a bit of the reformer in anyone who enters journalism. . . . And reformers are always going to make conservatives uncomfortable."[21]

Cunningham's bottom line is that journalists need to be willing to "adjudicate factual disputes."[22] Journalists should never allow the fear that others will call them biased to interfere with their own independent interpretations of and opinions about the news. To support his point, he quotes a lecture that Bill Marimow, *Baltimore Sun* editor, gave to Columbia students in which he said, "We want our reporters to be analysts."[23] Cunningham's example of an A+ headline is one that appeared in the *Washington Post*: "Bush Clings to Dubious Allegations."

Cunningham disclaims that he is advocating scrapping objectivity altogether. He simply says that journalists need to redefine it so as not to "trip them up" in the pursuit of "truth." The problem with this analysis is not his critique of the concept (he makes a number of good points), but rather his concept that "truth" is really just whatever an individual reporter makes it out to be. Add to this academia's dogma of relativism, moral or otherwise, and you have a recipe for disaster. Why is there any surprise over all the recent cases of fabrication and plagiarism at major papers and periodicals?

Neither is Cunningham advocating a return to the so-called European press, which is characterized by unabashed partisanship and was dominant in early America. He does not necessarily like objectivity, but he realizes that mainstream media would be out of their minds to let honest party labels stick—at the risk of losing a good part of their audiences. In an August 2004 *Editor & Publisher* article, Charles Geraci describes the philosophy of Boston University's journalism department chair, Robert Zelnick, and writes, "Zelnick says that the students don't care much about politics but there are values they hold dear, including environmental protection, gay rights, and a woman's right to an abortion."[24] One wonders how these issues can possibly be considered nonpolitical.

Marvin Olasky, editor of *World* and a professor at the University of Texas at Austin (one of the rare gems in such a place), critiques the standard ideology of objectivity with the same fervor as Cunningham. What he advocates replacing it with, however, is the polar opposite of Cunningham's suggestion. Olasky writes that biblical objectivity is "commitment to proclaiming God's objective truth as far as we know it."[25] Rather than assuming that the "truth" of each issue is relative, the Christian journalist should wholly reject yielding to a practice of "balancing subjectivities" in areas where the Bible speaks clearly.[26]

We might note that the degree to which this truth can be expressed in a venue that is not explicitly Christian will vary. Most publications in the secular mainstream press would not be thrilled by a front-page news report (rather than an op-ed) that described homosexuality as sin. Les Sillars, director of Patrick Henry College's journalism program, says that the audience of a given article must be taken into account. Where the audience exhibits consensus on the relevant issue, there is less of a need to be "balanced" in representing opposing sides. While a Christian writing for the *New York Times* would probably not quote the Bible in a news article, his view of right and wrong and good and evil should still inform his search for that which is true.

It is one thing for a Christian journalist writing for an obviously Christian magazine like *World* to be more willing to quote and consider straightforward Christian ideas. That is not lacking in objectivity; it is simply writing for a particular audience. But just as a Christian journalist for a secular publication should consider the fact that non-Christians are reading his writing, so too a secular reporter should recognize that his audience includes a lot of religious people who may be offended if he ignores their views and sensibilities.

The reason many journalists think they are being objective, despite the howls of protests from the Christian community, is that they simply don't know any people who are born-again Christians.

I remember being the subject of an *Atlantic Monthly* article in the early 1980s that described my appearance at a National Writer's Guild meeting in New York City. I was there to debate Kurt Vonegut, the famed novelist. The *Atlantic* described the audience's astonished reaction to my appearance, saying of the writers, "They had never seen such people"—meaning they had never met born-again Christians.

Far too often journalists live in a multicultural cocoon. They know all kinds of people who dominate big cities, but they know few born-again Christians and other cultural conservatives. Just remember the red and blue election map showing John Kerry's dominance in urban areas, while

President Bush dominated the vast majority of the total area of the United States. Major journalists almost always live in those urban cocoons and have no ability to understand those of us in the rest of America. Likewise, major universities are also smack in the middle of urban America.

In the face of the constant cry of bias, some leaders in the field now discredit the idea of "objectivity." The growing trend is for journalists-in-training to be instructed to intentionally filter news through their own personal analyses, unchained from any sort of standard of truth besides the ever-shifting "ethics" of the profession. Thus, it is only natural for these students to reflect the "truths" of their teachers—and when we look at what constitutes those "truths," we have every reason to be concerned.

Academic Activists—Not Professors of Professionalism: Today's Journalism Instructors

The leftist philosophies that seem to prevail in history and law departments inevitably affect J-school students as well. For that reason, there is no need to rehearse the standard ideologies of diversity, progressivism, and such again in this chapter. A few highlights are nevertheless in order.

As we attempted to get a handle on the practices in top journalism schools, we focused on three particular colleges. Where are they coming from? How can you tell?

One of the ways is to find where these professors have outside consulting roles as associate editors or writers for various publications. You will search in vain for a Columbia faculty member who writes for a conservative publication like the *National Review* or the *Weekly Standard*. However, you will find a substantial number of professors who are contributors to and editors of *The Nation*, the *New Republic*, *Mother Jones*, *Playboy*, and *Dissent*. These publications characterize themselves generally as "progressive left," which means that traditional Democrats are too centrist "the rabid right and its allies in the White House" are a threat to everything good about America.[27] "God Bless Atheism," an actual headline, serves as a suitable description of the genre.[28]

At Columbia, Todd Gitlin is a professor of journalism and sociology. He was educated at Harvard, the University of Michigan, and UC Berkeley. Gitlin is on the editorial board of *Dissent*, which describes itself as "rank[ing] among the handful of political journals read most regularly by U.S. intellectuals" and a magazine of both "the left" and "independent minds."[29] When referring to conservatives, Gitlin uses terms such as "fundamentalist Protestant legions" and "crackpot right."[30] One of his most recent books is *Letters to a Young Activist*, which draws on his own experience as a campus activist during the 1960s and advises left-leaning students on how to mobilize to accomplish such goals as universal health care.

Before becoming an associate professor in the magazine program at Northwestern University, Douglas Foster was the director of the Graduate School of Journalism at UC Berkeley. He is also the former editor in chief of *Mother Jones*, a publication that current editor Roger Cohn puts in the same genre as *The Nation*, only with less of an emphasis on opinionated commentary and more on reporting that "comes out from a liberal or progressive bent."[31] In an interview in the *Northwestern Chronicle*, Foster said that the "wild card" of the 2004 presidential elections is a toss-up between the events of September 11 and the fact that "the country has suffered terrorist attacks before from internal right-wing groups."[32] (Unsurprisingly, he noted that he liked "almost all" of the Democratic presidential primary candidates at the time.) Foster also likes covering animal behavior and comments that "chimpanzee politics aren't that different from ours"—and this is not a joke.[33] Understanding "our primate cousins," according to Foster, could be "a step toward outlining the evolution of our own moral codes."[34]

At the University of Wisconsin at Madison, Joel Rogers teaches Contemporary American Society, which fulfills one of the introductory social science requirements for journalism majors. Rogers is a veteran social activist and was named "one of the 100 Americans most likely to affect U.S. politics and culture in the 21st century" by *Newsweek*.[35] He currently earns this title partly as director of the Center on Wisconsin Strategy (COWS), a "progressive" think tank, and partly as the brains behind PROPAC, the "recruitment and training program" of the Progressive Majority (a liberal advocacy group started by the late Senator Paul Wellstone). As is the case with most prestigious journalist professors, Rogers is a contributing editor to *The Nation* and *Boston Review*. In an open letter on *Boston Review*'s New Democracy Forum, Rogers and his coeditor, Joshua Cohen, announce:

> Our convictions are egalitarian, radical democratic, and culturally pluralist. We want a world with greater socio-economic equality, in which life chances do not reflect the morally irrelevant differences among us. We want a world with more participation by citizens in running their common

affairs, in which the exercise of political power is shaped by our common reason rather than accumulations of private resources. And we want a world in which equal citizens acknowledge the diversity of decent ways to live, rather than seek to fit all human life into a single authoritative pattern.[36]
Enough said.

These are the people teaching the university graduates who "take their college perspectives to their jobs" as they report news to America.

Now you know why Dan Rather and company are not castigated for their use of fabricated documents against President Bush. Their college perspectives do not give them any reason to see a problem.

We should train our young people to write so well that they will appear as stars in a dark field. We should purpose to race to the top, not run away from the field of journalism.

CHAPTER 7

The Patriarchs of American Education: Colleges in the Early Republic

Higher education has not always been this way. The same group of prestigious schools that produce many of today's judges, senators, and presidents did the same in centuries past. Harvard, Yale, Princeton, and Columbia count John Hancock, John Adams, James Madison, Joseph Warren, John Jay, Luther Martin, Oliver Ellsworth, Gouverneur Morris, Noah Webster, and John Quincy Adams in their ranks of alumni. Likewise, Daniel Webster, Salmon P. Chase, and William McGuffey were graduates of schools where God was still at the center of a classical curriculum. The Harvard of John Adams's college years, however, was of a decidedly different character from the Harvard of today.

This chapter will take a step into history to examine American institutions of higher education from the nation's founding to the mid-nineteenth century. The bottom line, as you will see, is that philosophies of life and education at such schools started out very well indeed. Nevertheless, they have obviously performed an about-face and marched on a steadily downward path, sinking to present levels. Even though the 1996 anthology *Finding God at Harvard*

123

indicates that some there still seek Him,[1] the university as a whole has, quite literally, edited Him out. Harvard's Charter of 1650 began,

> Whereas through the good hand of God many well devoted persons have been and daily are moved and stirred up to give and bestow sundry gifts, legacies, lands, and revenues for the advancement of all good literature, arts and sciences in Harvard College in Cambridge in the County of Middlesex and to the maintenance of the President and Fellows and for all accommodations of buildings and all other necessary provisions that may conduce to the education of the English & Indian youth of this Country in knowledge: and godliness.[2]

This 1650 preamble was abridged for insertion into Harvard's current mission statement, adopted in 1997. Now it says, "In brief: Harvard strives to create knowledge, to open the minds of students to that knowledge, and to enable students to take best advantage of the educational opportunities."[3]

Two things are remarkable about Harvard's current mission statement. First, there is the obvious deletion of God from the institution's life and purposes. There is a second, more subtle shift. Today Harvard says that it creates knowledge. This presents a stark contrast to a previous Harvard code of laws which read, "Every one shall consider the main End of his life and studies to know God and Jesus Christ which is eternal life. . . . Seeing the Lord giveth wisdom, every one shall seriously by prayer in secret, seek wisdom of Him."[4] In a similar manner, Jeremiah Day, the longtime president of Yale, told his students, "Reason conducts us to the infinite fountain of knowledge, but does not itself discover the truths which are made known by inspiration. These are to be received on the simple testimony of God."[5]

The colleges and universities of today may have the same names, locations, and even a few of the same buildings as the colleges of the early 1800s, but there is a marked difference in foundational philosophy. Now man proclaims himself the author of knowledge. In the past, man understood his relationship to God and His omniscience more correctly.

Higher Education . . . Then

The first half of the nineteenth century was, as one author wrote a century later, the "heyday" of the American college.[6] In retrospect perhaps it was. Instead of taking classes entitled "Socio-cultural Transformation of Gender and Sexuality in the Modern Middle East" and "Gender and African History," students typically translated Homer, Plato, and Aristotle from the Greek and used Euclid to learn geometry.[7] History began with five books of Livy and Tacitus's histories—in their original Latin—followed by a more modern text that not only truthfully reported the facts but also warned of the "errors incident to the mind unenlightened by revealed religion."[8] Professors, rather than comparing the evidence for the existence of God to be similar to that for space aliens or werewolves, explained in their chemistry, geology, physics, and astronomy courses that "all these facts in the natural connection proclaim aloud the One God, whom man may know, adore, and love."[9] Faculty published books called *Evidences of Christianity* and *American and English Documents of the Constitution*—a far cry from today's titles, such as *Toward a Feminist Theory of the State* and *Gay New York: Gender, Urban Culture, and the Making of the Gay*

Male World, 1890–1940.[10] Tutors heard recitations on students' readings of William Paley's *Natural Theology* instead of inviting them to discuss why it was "de rigeur in the 1960s for left-leaning biologists to dress down."[11] And the college president explained to students in chapel services that "the conservation of society can be trusted only to moral and religious forces," rather than concurring with the director of the school's Lesbian, Gay, Bisexual and Transsexual Life Center that she should "permit the celebration of same-sex unions in Duke [University] Chapel."[12]

Colleges of the mid-nineteenth century differed little from their predecessors two hundred years before.[13] From their founding era in the 1600s until the Civil War, daily chapel was still mandatory, presidents were still clergymen, and the purposes and goals of education remained the same. The classics dominated the curriculum as they had since the start. Governance may have shifted from guilds of scholars to boards of trustees, but internal methodologies of teaching and discipline changed only slightly in the process.[14]

Through the colonial era and the early days of our constitutional republic, these colleges tended to possess a certain fundamental character that was preserved through the influx of colonial settlers, multiple wars, and the development of a distinctly American culture. This consistency flowed naturally from the common motive that these institutions shared at the time of their founding. As Frederick Rudolph writes in *The American College and University*, these colleges began as a purposeful "planting of temples of piety and intellect in the wilderness."[15] They were explicitly religious, though they aspired to provide men of culture who would bridge the gap between the civilization of the Old World and the barbarism of the New.[16]

Freshman and sophomores generally spent their days learning habits of mental discipline by translating Greek and Latin, working through mathematics, and learning the principles of grammar, logic, and rhetoric.[17] Natural philosophy and higher, applied mathematics filled the majority of the junior year. Christianity was not absent from these more technical studies but interwoven throughout. Presidents and professors did their best to cultivate the hearts of their students. The trustees of the College of New Jersey (now Princeton) named as one of their two objectives, "to rectify the Heart [of each student], by inculcating the great Precepts of *Christianity*."[18] As we will see, the driving force behind it all was a passion for truth, love for God, and dedication to virtue.

The pinnacle of the curriculum at American colleges during that bygone era was Moral Philosophy. In this capstone course, normally taught by the president of the college to the senior class, the mental discipline instilled in students through prior years of rigorous instruction in the classics was used to apply the truths of the universe—biblical revelation—to every area of life. In fact, it was not until the latter part of the nineteenth century that history and government were established as independent disciplines. This simple fact reflected a consensus among professors and college administrators that there is but one overarching objective of any form of education: the development of a moral and virtuous people. This goal, in turn, reflected a worldview in which life was understood as one seamless whole rather than fractured parts. History, government, economics, philosophy, and science were all subjected to the same, unchangeable plumb line of Judeo-Christian ethics.

Of course, there were disagreements as to what that plumb line meant for daily living, and we would be deceiving ourselves if we thought that these colleges accomplished their goals and fulfilled their ideals perfectly. Men have never been angels. Even in the 1740s, George Whitefield frowned on Harvard's increasingly liberal reputation.[19] Two decades later, when Harvard faculty allowed students to choose Christ Church in Cambridge over the Congregational meetinghouse for Sunday worship, contemporaries worried that it fostered "religious irresponsibility."[20] Yale was founded in 1701 over concerns that Harvard might be on the downward path theologically, and then the College of New Jersey was started in 1746 for the same reason in regard to Yale. Students even then were prone to small rebellions over such things as college food.[21] None of this, however, undermines the fact that until after the 1850s, academic programs as well as student behavior and standards of religious orthodoxy were "mediated through the American Protestant heritage."[22] Furthermore, revivals were a frequent means of restoration. Events always transpired that, for a period, kept the schools chained to their Christian foundations. For example, Yale president Timothy Dwight fired any faculty member who championed French rationalism around the turn of the nineteenth century. There was much that these schools did right for nearly two centuries, and to glean from their successes is not the same as looking wistfully through rose-colored glasses.

We began our overview of present-day American collegiate education by examining one of the most popular college history texts today, the Marxist tome by Howard Zinn. Accordingly, it is appropriate to look at some of the most widely used college history texts from the classical era of

American higher education to see the true magnitude of the shift in higher education.

America According to Tytler and Smyth

Imagine for a moment how you would perceive your role as a national leader if your study of history had taught you the following about states and their statesmen:

Some nations have enjoyed, during the course of many ages, an unvarying and uninterrupted prosperity; while others have been destined to a short, unfortunate, and despicable mediocrity. . . . But while we contemplate their changes of fortune, their prosperity, their disgraces, their revolutions, and their final catastrophe, must these vicissitudes be considered only as the effects of a blind fatality? . . . No, certainly. . . . "Accustom your mind," said the excellent Phocion to Aristias, "to discern in the prosperity of nations that recompense which the Author of Nature has affixed to the practice of virtue; and in their adversity, the chastisement which he has thought proper to bestow on vice." No state ever ceased to be prosperous, but in consequence of having departed from those institutions to which she owed her prosperity.[23]

This passage reveals a worldview that sees history as driven by factors unlike the class warfare discovered by Marx and repackaged by Zinn. Nations are not driven by class warfare or the ideology of fatalistic materialism. A nation's virtue determines its destiny.

It is immediately obvious that this quotation is from a different era. This passage was taken from one of the two great history texts of the early 1800s, *Elements of General History* written by Alexander Fraser Tytler. He was a professor of history at the University of Edinburgh in Scotland prior to the turn of the nineteenth century. The earliest catalogs available from both Harvard and Yale name his *Elements of General History* as the operative history text over many editions and a span of many years.[24]

The second great text was William Smyth's *Lectures on Modern History: From the Irruption of the Northern Nation to the Close of the American Revolution.* An 1887 documentary report on the study of history in American institutions of higher education described the many editions of William Smyth's *Lectures* as the *vade mecum* (i.e., constant reference tool, Latin for "go with me") of many Harvard students for decades beginning in the 1830s.[25] How did Smyth treat the founding fathers? Did he see them as rapacious villains like our "friend" Howard Zinn? Smyth said the following about the motivation of the Founding Fathers in launching the movement for American independence:

> But, on the whole, the general enthusiasm that was excited by this single principle, the fundamental principle of the American controversy, that the parliament of Great Britain had no right to tax them, is quite unexampled in history; and that men should act on the foresight and expectation of events, just as if the events were present . . . is a perfect phenomenon in the records of the world, and a very curious specimen of that reasoning, sagacious, spirited, determined attachment to the principles of civil liberty.[26]

This laudatory perspective does not spring from idealized patriotism. Its author, Smyth, was an Englishman—

a professor at the University of Cambridge. Both Tytler and Smyth judged the Founders' campaign for liberty to be sincere and remarkable in human history, not a façade which masked their personal and corporate greed.

Rather than castigating George Washington as a selfish supporter of the Constitution—a document created to benefit his own socioeconomic class—Smyth instead concluded that the first president was selflessly noble:

> [Washington] *enabled* his country to stand aloof
> from the unhappy storm of European politics; he re-
> signed his popularity to accomplish so great an end;
> and he maintained the constitution over which he
> presided by a serene and dignified confidence in its
> merits, and a calm exercise of its acknowledged
> powers and authority.[27]

Smyth gave evidence of the veracity of Washington's now-famous query, "Can it be . . . that Providence has not connected the permanent felicity of a nation with its virtue?"[28]

Unity. Providence. Virtue. Liberty. Patriotism. These were the themes that dominated both the textbooks and faculties in early America. They shaped the character, culture, and ideals of many generations of students in a manner that is essentially the polar opposite of today's prevailing philosophies.

Unity of Life, Unity of Knowledge

The concept of diversity in its modern sense would have been foreign to colleges two hundred years ago. Instead, *unity* was the emphasis. This does not refer to cultural uniformity, socioeconomic equality, or a cult of white, European males. Nor does it mean sitting in a circle, holding hands, and corporately meditating to enhance mutual self-esteem. No, it describes the predominant characteristic of a world-view in which there is but one standard of measure: God Himself, as revealed in His Word and His world. Every subject matter reached a common conclusion; all truth points to God.

Indeed, the discovery of truth—not its creation—was at the core of this unity. One historian explains, "When scholars discovered truth, they showed that scholarly activity had a common purpose, and they informed human history, the natural world, and contemporary culture with a single theistic value system."[29] Reason and revelation were not at odds, and neither were faith and science. In the words of a minister associated with Yale professors during the 1800s, it is the "very spirit of true science that finds truth in facts—God's truth in God's facts."[30] Properly applied science would always point to the Creator. Francis Bowen, the well-known Alford Professor of Natural Religion, Moral Philosophy, and Civil Polity at Harvard, wrote in his book *The Principles of Metaphysical and Ethical Science Applied to the Evidences of Religion:*

> I have no fears for the security of the theist's faith, when it rests on the same basis with all the doctrines of natural science. . . . To distrust such evidence, or to be incapable of acting upon it, is the common test of the folly that borders upon idiocy; and to such an unbeliever, therefore, may be literally applied the words of Scripture, "The fool hath said in his heart, There is no God."[31]

This view of Christianity in society has been completely reversed. In the early Republic, those who rejected Christianity were viewed as possessing "folly that borders upon idiocy." The *Washington Post* recently characterized Christians in remarkably similar terms, describing conservative Christians as "poor, uneducated, and easy to command."[32]

Let's reflect a moment longer on the difference between Francis Bowen of 1855 and the *Washington Post* of 1993. Both consider those who reject their philosophy as essentially uneducated. It would be inaccurate to say that critics of either Bowen or the *Post* were, in fact, untaught persons. Rather, there is a deeper criticism that cuts to a philosophical point. A person who has book-learning yet who rejects the fundamental philosophy of the day is considered "uneducated" by the educators. In Bowen's time those who rejected Christianity were viewed as lacking common sense and wisdom. Today it is those who *embrace* Christianity who bear the brunt of such epithets. To be considered wise, one must embrace a philosophy that underlies the system of instruction.

Bowen's philosophy was the standard in the 1800s, not the exception. Mark Hopkins at Williams College was also an educator of great stature. His educational methodology was also typical of the era. After presenting a lengthy sequence of arguments that defended the truths of Christianity and formed a cohesive moral philosophy, he "turned to the real grist of the course—application of this system to all phases of life."[33] This included everything from economics to government to character-building. Coherence was possible because the standard by which philosophies were judged was not man-made. The existence of absolutes was not a matter of debate or merely an interesting question. While there was still a great deal of room to determine the proper application of truth, the fact that "moral awareness transcended everything" enabled Hopkins's teachings to form a "truly integrated course."[34]

Unity was also evident in the curriculum as a whole. A college education was seen as a broad building block upon which hands-on, more discipline-specific training could later be built. *The Yale Report* of 1828 described and defended the classical approach to college instruction that had been in use since early colonial days.[35] The purpose of classical languages, ancient literature, mathematics, logic, philosophy, history, and rhetoric was to teach students first how to *reason* and *think*, then how to *apply the facts* of the world and *express them* with eloquence in both writing and speech. These are skills that every productive citizen and leading member of society would need. It sounds so common-sense that we might wonder why anyone would object, yet the critics had already begun to harp against such an approach to higher education.

A college education can sometimes seem like a randomly organized smorgasbord of facts, theories, and courses. This is what made the Moral Philosophy course, chapel and church services, and campus standards of behavior so important. Education was designed to develop human beings who embraced and advanced a specific theistic philosophy of life.

Faculty and students were expected to walk in integrity whether they were translating Cicero and rehearsing Euclid's second postulate, eating in the dining commons, or joining for prayer and Scripture reading in the "College-Hall" every morning and evening.[36] They were to "Live Religious, Godly and Blameless Lives, according to the Rules of Gods Word, diligently Reading the holy Scriptures the Fountain of Light and Truth; and constantly attend upon all the Duties of Religion both in Publick and Secret."[37]

Such goals for education are possible only when one begins with God.

Teaching Under God

It has already become clear that these early college faculties believed in God—and not just in an abstract, deist sense. In fact, it is a tired fallacy to claim that deists controlled America at its founding, a view commonly taught in today's colleges and universities. Consider one such claim by Gordon S. Wood, a professor of history at the Ivy League's Brown University:

As several of these commentators suggest, religion was important to Americans, but most to ordinary people, not to *the educated elite* of the Founding Fathers (although some of them did turn to Christianity out of despair late in their lives). Many of the founders were deists, or who today we might call "secular humanists."[38] (Emphasis added)

Such historical analysis is wishful thinking for at least two reasons. First, top-ranked scholars like James Hutson of the Library of Congress discredit the notion that men like Hamilton and Washington (whom Wood specifically cites) were deists.[39] Hutson undertook a thorough review of the respective influences of deism and evangelical Christianity in the late 1700s in America and concluded that "evangelicalism demolished deism in eighteenth-century America."[40]

The second reason that Wood's typical deism claim rings untrue goes beyond the endless debates about the lives of the Founders themselves. To determine the veracity of Wood's claim that the educated elite, including the founders, were deists, one need only look at the elite colleges. Ivy League professors today seem loath to believe that their predecessors in office were thoroughly Christian. The only members of the elite who were Christians, they assert, were those who had a pitiable relapse into faith when their circumstances of life proved difficult toward the end of life. Yet the evidence is starkly to the contrary. Elite schools were dominated by orthodox, evangelical Christians. American colleges during the revolutionary era and early Republic believed in a living God who reveals himself in the Bible, not a divine watchmaker who left men basically to themselves.

Christian professors of the early Republic would eschew today's academic arrogance. They would not imagine claiming the ability to create knowledge, as Harvard today claims. Nor would they be tempted to believe that they could explain everything, as contemporary Enlightenment philosophers were prone to believe. Like Jeremiah Day, who was affiliated with Yale for nearly seventy years in positions ranging from tutor to president, these professors allowed room for the supernatural. Day gave a sermon in which he said:

> Here is the distinction between faith and mere reason. Not that faith, in divine testimony is *opposed* to reason. But the objects of faith are frequently *above* unassisted reason. The highest efforts of the human mind could not reach them without a revelation from heaven. . . . But God is to be believed, when He speaks to us; whether we can or cannot trace the connection between His declarations and the operations of His hands.[41]

Some may call this blind faith, but they should remember that these are the same people who devoted a significant part of their curriculum to apologetics-related topics and wrote and used treatises such as *Evidences of Christianity, Evidences of the Existence and Attributes of the Deity,* and *The Principles of Metaphysical and Ethical Science Applied to the Evidences of Religion*.[42] Few twenty-first-century

Christians could defend their faith so thoroughly and with practiced rhetorical skill.

A high view of God is also evident into the popular textbooks of Francis Wayland, Brown University president from 1827 to 1855. His *Elements of Moral Science* incorporates the core message of the gospel into a discussion of the role of conscience, the components of prayer, and the nature of individual liberty:

> It is that Infinite Being, who stands to us in the relation of Creator, Preserver, Benefactor, Lawgiver, and Judge; and to whom we stand in the relation of dependent, helpless, ignorant, and sinful creatures. . . . By virtue of the relation which he sustains to the creation, he is the Protector, Ruler, and Proprietor of all, we are under obligations to obey him in every thing.
>
> He, therefore, has revealed himself to us in the relation of a Savior and Redeemer, a God forgiving transgression and iniquity; and thus, by all the power of this new relation, he imposes upon us new obligations to gratitude, repentance, and love. . . .
>
> Now, since, as we have before shown, the light of conscience and the dictates of natural religion are insufficient to exert the requisite moral power over man, our only hope is in that revelation of his will which God has made in the Holy Scriptures.[43]

Wayland's text follows the typical *modus operandi* of moral philosophy courses. It starts by proposing a methodology through which the discussion is to function, then proceeds to build a foundation centered on observations about human nature. After this, the author elaborates on a "generalized ethical teaching" or "dictum of action." He concludes by showing how the "law" just framed should be applied to everything from marriage to forms of government.[44] Nowhere was the Law of Nature, or Nature's God, considered irrelevant.

And, in a manner that we have seen before, religious philosophies inevitably affect practical morality.

When Evil Is Called Evil

The Allegheny College board of trustees declared in 1833 that "practical morality, and the best interests of man, in time and eternity, are intimately dependent on the belief and influence of the principles of revealed religion, that a system of education leaving them out of view would be materially defective."[45] In their day this was merely a restatement of what was already commonly held. Since a nation's liberty and prosperity were believed to be intimately connected with the objective character of its people, these trustees chose to make character development the most important factor in ensuring not only the success of their school but also their country. It was not that academics was unimportant—quite the contrary—but Christianity and properly ordered lives were more than just means to achieve an academically successful end. They *were* the end, and education helped the process. To reiterate the passage from the Harvard code, "Every one shall consider the main End of his life and studies to know God and Jesus Christ which is eternal life."

A similar emphasis appears in a South Carolina College inaugural address given by Francis Lieber in 1835. He was a prolific author, renowned intellectual, and history and "political economy" professor at both South Carolina College

and Columbia College (now University, in New York). He
said:

> The great object of education must always re-
> main the cultivation of the heart and the head, of,
> in other words, a moral and intellectual cultivation.
> The latter, or scientific education, ought again to
> consist of training and storing the mind—of storing
> it with sound knowledge and of training it in the
> habit of correct thought. . . .
>
> This important end, the moral cultivation of the
> student, is in the power of every science taught in
> the college to promote; mathematics, the natural
> sciences, philology by no means excepted; but to the
> province of none it belongs so peculiarly as to the
> science which you have assigned to me, constantly
> to direct the mind of the student to the best and
> surest principles upon which human society is
> founded, or for which nations have contended, to
> the conspicuous examples of virtue or vice, to the
> safe operation of wise laws, or the detrimental
> course which cunning or fell ambition, short-sighted
> cowardice, and careless or intentional disregard of
> right and duty, always take with individuals as well
> as with whole communities and nations.[46]

Even with matters of political economy, virtue was bigger than test grades. Lieber knew that students with this
kind of character and this kind of vision would be prepared
to do great things and also that academic excellence would
typically follow.

How did those colleges cultivate morality? First, instructors led by example. Regardless of the focus of their specific
discipline, they "were themselves sincere and earnest

Christians," and presidents in particular were often ministers.[47] Second, they led by discipline and precept. Not only
did the rigorous workload leave little time for dallying
and play, but faculties also saw the character development
of their students as a part of their personal responsibili-
ties.[48] Harvard students in the 1850s were taught from
William Whewell's two-volume *Elements of Morality*,[49]
which instructed:

> The moral precepts just stated: Be not angry:
> Bear no malice: Do not covet: Do not lie: Do not de-
> ceive: Do not lust: Do not desire to break Law: are
> to be applied to the whole train of our affections, de-
> sires, thoughts, and purposes, and to the whole
> course of actions, internal and external, which
> make up our lives.[50]

Other topics included range from sexual purity to homi-
cide and rights of property, and the tome ends with a section
entitled "Moral Education Requires Religious Education."
Once again we see that God was inextricably linked to this
system of ethics. Francis Wayland wrote, "Such is the case
with marriage. This is a form of society established by God.
Men have no right to enter into it as they please, but only according to the laws which God has established; and, if they
act otherwise, mutual misery will be the result."[51]

According to these professors, family, school, and government were united to accomplish the same end of developing
a moral people who saw no disparity between their public
and private lives.[52] Academia continued what the family
had begun, and government contributed to the process by
allowing the other two to do their job.[53] Students were expected to enter college with a "Sufficient Testamony [*sic*] of
his Blameless and inoffensive Life."[54] College presidents

were quick to affirm, "You can send us your boys, this grand old college will keep the faith."[55]

A perfect example is again found in the text of Alexander Fraser Tytler. He explains that the strength of the early Roman republic derived from the work ethic and virtuous manners of its populace.[56] This kind of character alone, he says, is able to support a free form of government. What is the secret to achieving such strength? Tytler answers: (1) fathers, who although they held the *jus vitae et necis* (the right of life and death) over their households, were affectionate and benevolent in the use of their power, and (2) mothers who possessed a jealous concern for the education and internal growth of their own children. No laws prescribed this system or mandated adherence, yet it was accomplished with success. It was only when parental authority was "weakened and abridged" that corruption took root and spread.[57]

We might wish again for a day when neither family and college nor family and government were at odds. Pro-family really meant pro-family back then. And professors did place a premium on freedom, but it was the freedom to be responsible rather than lazy and licentious.

Measuring Progress

We discussed in the third chapter how many professors today describe "progress." In early America, the prevailing philosophy called for self-restricted moral citizens and a constitutionally restrained government as the keys to freedom. But today unrestrained passions and unrestrained government providers are seen as the means to achieve utopia. In the minds of today's professors such as Peggy Cooper Davis and Jennifer Hochschild, any government is a failure if it does not, on the one hand, talk of liberty while forcing sexual deviancy into prominence and, on the other, talk of compassion while taxing and controlling its citizens to no end. A vice-ridden nation with a gargantuan government would not seem like a uptopia to the founders.

Progress according to Francis Bowen had different implications. He wrote in *The Principles of Political Economy Applied to the Condition, the Resources, and the Institutions of the American People* that the government is best that fulfills God's design the most. This involves stepping aside to let His creation take its course, so long as "vice and crime" do not frustrate His intent.[58] As you read this passage, imagine how Bowen would respond to a scheme including government-subsidized vacations and cradle-to-grave care:

> Society is a complex and delicate machine, the real Author and Governor of which is divine. . . . Man cannot interfere with His work without marring it. The attempts of legislators to turn the industry of society in one direction or another, out of its natural and self-chosen channels . . . are almost invariably productive of harm. Laissez-faire; "these things regulate themselves," in common phrase; which means, of course, that God regulates them by his general laws, which always, in the long run, work to good. In these modern days, the ruler or governor who is most to be dreaded is, not the tyrant, but the busybody. Let the course of trade and the condition of society alone, is the best advice which can be given to the legislator, the projector, and the reformer. Busy yourselves, if you must be busy, with individual cases of wrong, hardship, or

suffering; but do not meddle with the general laws of the universe.[59]

The legislator fulfills his job by framing human laws that rarely "require an active obedience," but rather are "designed to prevent such action on the part of the few as would impede or limit the healthful action of the many."[60] Regulatory schemes, when they exist, are supposed to place a premium on freedom. It is little wonder that American liberty was so firmly and deeply grounded when the first generations of leaders received such instruction.

In the same spirit as Bowen, William Smyth names government nannyhood as Britain's chief mistake in dealing with its American colonies. Its statesmen, he explains, were ignorant and inattentive to the "great leading principles of political economy," including free trade.[61] They were blind in their attempt to "break the American spirit," since it was that very thing that created the nation.[62] This spirit loved freedom, but it was also dependent on the character, restraint, and ethic of each person. Government was prone to reflect the will of the people, either for good or for evil.

Professors did not shy away from conveying to their students the sense that the future direction of the nation was in their hands. Each individual's willingness to turn from or to selfish and sinful indulgence would determine their corporate course. The profound weight of this responsibility could not help but push these young citizens on to excellence. One college president put it well when he said:

God has rendered the blessing of freedom inseparable from moral restraint in the individual; and hence it is vain for a people to expect to be free, unless they are first willing to be virtuous. It is on this point that the question of the permanency of the present form of government of the United States turns. . . . There is no self-sustaining power in any form of social organization. The only self-sustaining power is in individual virtue. And the form of a government will always adjust itself to the moral condition of a people. A virtuous people will, by their own moral power, frown away oppression, and, under any form of constitution, become essentially free. A people surrendered up to their own licentious passions, must be held in subjection by force.[63]

"Your personal responsibility," we hear, "far from being a hindrance, is what will enable America to be free." This sober message clashes harshly with the messages students hear today, such as, "Do what pleases *you* now," "Traditional sexual mores should be nonexistent," and "A traditional capitalist work ethic does nothing but hinder my social welfare scheme."

While today's "progressive" professors may be perceptive in realizing that live-and-let-live attitudes in moral arenas necessarily require greater government supervision in other areas, they are far from attaining the acumen of those of the past who said that there are two factors that ultimately contribute to progress: wisdom and truth.[64]

The Christian Patriot

The distinguished vice president of the College of New Jersey, Philip Lindsley, declared in 1837: "[Students] may be Methodists, Presbyterians, Baptists, Episcopalians, Roman Catholics, Quakers—Whigs, Democrats, Federalists, Conservatives—we care not—so that they are Christians and patriots."[65] Christians and patriots. That was all that was needed. It was on these two core characteristics that early American professors could build the skills that students needed to succeed.

As we have also seen, however, this kind of spirit is precisely what modern academia is attempting to extinguish. Tytler taught the leaders of the young Republic that there was a clear connection between virtue and patriotism—both of which are essential to the preservation of liberty:

> The love of liberty, or the passion for national freedom, is a noble, a disinterested, and a virtuous feeling. Where this feeling is found to prevail in any great degree, it is a proof that the manners of that community are yet pure and unadulterated; for corruption of manners infallibly extinguishes the patriotic spirit. In a nation confessedly corrupted, there is often found a prevailing cry for liberty, which is heard the loudest among the most profligate of the community; but let us carefully distinguish *that* spirit from *virtuous patriotism*. . . . The aversion to restraint assumes the same external appearance with the love of liberty; but this criterion will enable us to distinguish the reality from the counterfeit. In fact the spirit of liberty and a general corruption of manners are so totally adverse and repugnant to each other, that it is utterly impossible they should have even the most transitory existence in the same age and nation. . . . On the other hand, while virtue remains in the manners of the people, no national misfortune is irretrievable, nor any political situation so desperate, that hope may not remain for a favorable change.[66]

Francis Lieber wrote in 1858 that professors in free countries—regardless of their century—*must* foster a "heightened public spirit, which loves and honors father and mother, and neighbors, and country; which makes us deeply feel for our country's glory and its faults; makes us willing to die, and, what is often far more difficult, to live for it; that patriotism which is consistent with St. Paul's command: Honor all men."[67] This is easy to say, hard to do. United States Senator Lamar Alexander (R-Tennessee) believes that unity still *does* "trump diversity" in America, even though most students at our educational institutions are fed a steady diet of multicultural bunk instead.[68] To make his point, he describes naturalization day in Tennessee, where immigrants still have to swear that they will "support and defend the Constitution and laws of the United States of America against all enemies, foreign and domestic" and "bear true faith and allegiance to the same." We have lost that spirit on our campuses, and it will not be painless gaining it back.

One notable law professor of yesteryear, Joseph Story, would have been sobered by the path that America's educators have chosen to take. He wrote extensive and authoritative commentaries on the legal principles and the Constitution with the hope that professors and students alike would take care to preserve their heritage. Story warned:

Let the American youth never forget, that they possess a noble inheritance, bought by the toils, and sufferings, and blood of their ancestors; and capable, if wisely improved, and faithfully guarded, of transmitting to their latest posterity all the substantial blessings of life, the peaceful enjoyment of liberty, property, religion, and independence. The structure has been erected by architects of consummate skill and fidelity; its foundations are solid; its compartments are beautiful, as well as useful; its arrangements are full of wisdom and order; and its defences are impregnable from without. It has been reared for immortality, if the work of man may justly aspire to such a title. It may, nevertheless, perish in an hour by the folly, or corruption, or negligence of its only keepers, THE PEOPLE.

Republics are created by the virtue, public spirit, and intelligence of the citizens. They fall, when the wise are banished from the public councils, because they dare to be honest, and the profligate are rewarded, because they flatter the people, in order to betray them.[69]

For a time both before and after Story's day, educators heeded the spirit of his warning. American youth *were* reminded of the legacy they inherited from their earliest colonial forefathers, they *were* impressed with the necessity of conducting a virtuous and upright life, and they *were* inspired to move their country forward with vision and wisdom. We can guess what kind of leaders this guidance produced for America, but let's take a closer look.

The Legacy of American Higher Education

As noted previously, the vast majority of individuals who directed America during its most formative years graduated from the same institutions that shape so many of our leaders today. Below are a few examples, though there are many more.

James Otis, described as one of the "three indispensable men" responsible for "stirring up the Revolution," graduated from Harvard in 1743.[70] He resigned as advocate-general of the colonial court system in order to defend the colonists after the British government issued their infamous writs of assistance. These writs authorized colonists' houses to be searched for smuggled goods without probable cause. His oration before authorities launched him into the public eye, and he used his influence to argue forcefully for independence. After being beaten over the head by British revenue officials, he suffered brain damage that was to remain with him for the rest of his life. America, however, did not soon forget his contributions to its liberty.

Another early patriot, John Hancock, also called Harvard his alma mater. This is the man who filled the presidential chair of the Continental Congress in 1776 and was the first to sign the Declaration of Independence, well aware that it might cost him his life. He was governor of Massachusetts during the uneasy era following the Constitutional Convention while the states debated about the merits of ratifying. Although "his character and motives were aspersed by the interested," a biographer noted half a century later, "when the agitation ceased, and the clouds passed away, his virtues and exalted character, shone with a purer lustre [*sic*] than before."[71]

John Adams—the determined voice for the colonists' rights, delegate to the Continental Congress, sponsor of the first motion "that the colonies should form governments *independent of the Crown*," drafter and signer of the Declaration, foreign minister, vice president under George Washington, and second president of the United States— was a third Harvard grad. David McCullough describes him as a "great-hearted, persevering man of uncommon ability and force" who was "both a devout Christian and independent thinker."[72]

King's College, now Columbia University, graduated John Jay in 1764. Among other things, Jay was appointed as the first chief justice under the newly adopted U.S. Constitution (he had previously held the same position in New York), served for a time as president of the Continental Congress and governor of New York, and authored some of the *Federalist Papers*. The Jay Treaty bears his name. Jay was a firm believer in the authority of the Bible and possessed a character that was "conscientious, upright, just, and wise."[73]

James Madison completed the undergraduate program at the College of New Jersey (Princeton) and pursued graduate studies in Hebrew, ethics, and theology for an additional year in the 1760s. The influence of this "Father of the Constitution" can hardly be understated. Besides working inexhaustibly at the Constitutional Convention, he later introduced the Bill of Rights in the new House of Representatives in 1791. He was also the fourth chief executive of the United States. His "impressive" mind and thoughts were described as "but decorations to set off to advantage his pure and incorruptible virtue and integrity."[74]

Other colonial patriots and signers of the Declaration of Independence or Constitution attended elite schools as well. Joseph Warren and Elbridge Gerry graduated from Harvard. William Johnson, Jared Ingersoll, and Abraham Baldwin did the same from Yale. Alexander Hamilton started attending King's College (now Columbia University) in 1773 but decided that he needed to cut his studies short in order to fight for America's independence. Gouverneur

Morris was a King's College grad. College of New Jersey alumni include Oliver Ellsworth, William Paterson, Gunning Bedford, Luther Martin, William Davies, and Alexander Martin.

Noah Webster graduated with the Yale class of 1778. His legendary 1828 dictionary not only provided Americans with a consistent standard for their language but also functioned as a "force for educating Americans in the principles of the Christian faith, principles that could remake government, schools, and other pertinent social institutions."[75] Although his true conversion did not occur until well after his Yale years, the training he received during that time forged his conviction that education would be the key to unlocking America's grand potential.

After the Revolution, John Quincy Adams followed in his father's footsteps and attended Harvard, graduating in 1787. He served as minister to the Netherlands, minister to Russia, U.S. Senator, and secretary of state under President James Monroe before his election as our sixth president. Adams returned to the House of Representatives in 1830, where he fought indefatigably against the "gag rule" until it was repealed after eight years and the House could no longer table antislavery petitions. He was another dedicated Christian with political integrity, courage, and independence "of a grade rarely seen."[76]

Daniel Webster was a student at Dartmouth from 1797 until his graduation in 1801. At that time Dartmouth had only been open about thirty years and was still faithful to its founder, Great Awakening evangelist and Yale graduate Eleazar Wheelock. It was also faithful to its mission, which is reflected in its motto, *vox clamantis in deserto* ("a voice crying in the wilderness"). Following a legal apprenticeship, he argued and won important precedent-setting cases in the Supreme Court including *Gibbons v. Ogden* and *McCullough v. Maryland*. This experience prepared him well to use his brilliant oratorical skills to preserve and defend federal union in the Senate, earning him the title of the "silver-tongued orator."

Another Dartmouth alumnus is Salmon P. Chase. Although seldom remembered today, Chase was one of the foremost antislavery advocates in his day as a senator, secretary of the treasury, and chief justice of the United States. One biographer writes of him, "No man of his time had a stronger conception of the moral issues involved in the Civil War; none showed greater courage and resolution. . . . The underlying idea of his public life was to bring the law up to the moral standards of the country, and to make both moral standards and law apply to black men as well as to white men."[77]

William Holmes McGuffey graduated from Washington College in 1826, the same year that Chase did from Dartmouth.[78] He was shaped by a classical Christian education and devoted his life to passing on that same form of education to the youth of America. McGuffey believed, like Noah Webster, that religion and education are inextricably linked both to each other and to the health of the nation. This conviction urged him on as he wrote his celebrated *Readers* for grade-school students, thoroughly infusing them with biblical values, and as he taught classical languages, lectured in moral philosophy, and gave chapel sermons at the many colleges with which he was associated.

Other early American leaders who did not attend elite schools often received a comparable education from a school in England or from dedicated parents who taught them at home. For example, George Mason, one of the chief figures responsible for making the adoption of the Constitution contingent on a bill of rights, received most of his education by poring through the books of a neighboring attorney's library and by learning about plantation management from his mother.[79] Another prominent Virginian statesman, Richard Henry Lee, was placed in an English school where he spent most of his time reading ancient history, thus becoming "early indoctrinated with the ideas of republicanism" and "principles of civil liberty."[80] Patrick Henry's father drew from his own educational experiences at King's College, Aberdeen (Scotland), to teach his son in the classics, while his mother nurtured his oratorical abilities by making him repeat sermons to her on the way home from church. When the "Voice of the Revolution" was a young man, he enjoyed reading Latin and Greek classics such as Livy's histories.[81] It is said that his exceptional skills and demeanor were, "if not originally inspired, at least highly raised, by the noble models set before him by this favourite author."[82]

Striving to Shine Forth

We can see in these brief biographies a common thread. A superior education grounded in Christianity and the classics gave our early statesmen the tools they needed to lead the new nation and shape the culture with skill. Fires were probably kindled in the hearts of students as they listened to their school's provost commission them at a 1757 graduation with the words:

Oh! then, let no Part of your future Conduct
disgrace the Lessons you have received, or disap-
point the Hopes you have so justly raised! Consider

yourselves, from this Day, as distinguished above
the Vulgar, and called upon to act a more important
Part in Life—Strive to shine forth in every Species
of *Moral Excellence*, and to support the Character
and Dignity of Beings formed for endless Duration.
The Christian World stands much in Need of inflex-
ible Patterns of *Integrity* and *public Virtue*; and no
Part of it more so than the Land you inhabit.

Remember that superior Talents demand a superior Exercise of every good Quality. . . . Unless
your Education is seen conspicuous in your Lives,
alas! what will be its Significancy to you, or to us?
Will it not be deemed rather to have been a vain
Art of furnishing the HEAD, than a true *Discipline*
of the HEART and MANNERS? . . .

What a Reproach would it be to have it said
that, under us, you had obtained all Sorts of
Learning, and yet had not obtained *Wisdom*—espe-
cially that *Wisdom*, which has for its *Beginning* the
FEAR OF GOD, and for its *End* EVERLASTING
FELICITY!

But we have every Reason to expect far better
Things of you.[83]

Indeed he did, and his hopes were not soon disappointed.

Great knowledge carries with it great responsibility.
When this burden was placed upon the shoulders of those
young students, the weight of glory served to push them
forward to greater heights, and they took America with
them.

CHAPTER 8

Restoring the Christian Mandate for Leadership

Christians cannot compare the early days of elite colleges with the degenerated practices of today without asking, "What do we do now?" Or to rephrase Francis Schaeffer, "How then should we educate Christian leaders?"

Several things are quick and easy to conclude.

For me and my house, my children will not attend these secularized colleges and universities to be subjected to indoctrination and ridicule leveled at them from an openly antagonistic Christian worldview. I will leave it to readers to reach their own decisions for their own families in this regard.

Why in the world would any born-again Christian give a single penny to a college that did not affirmatively embrace a biblical worldview? For that matter, why would any business give money to a college that systematically attacked free enterprise? Why would anyone fund their philosophical opponents?

But it is not enough to say what we will *not* do. What are the positive steps of action that we should take to give Christian young people a viable opportunity to receive the kind of education that cultivates a set of leaders with legitimacy in the eyes of the citizenry?

You cannot fight something with nothing. We cannot fight the Ivy League and other elite schools with Christian colleges that are aimed at educating a broad cross section of the community. It is a good and noble task to do this. The vast majority of secular colleges are focused on this kind of education, aimed at a broad range of student talent. For us to give the top Christian students the best possible opportunities, however, there must be a Christian equivalent of the Ivy League.

Is this even possible?

Yes, of course. I have four basic arguments to support this conclusion.

First, remember the history of the Ivy League. These were openly Christian colleges. And they were the top colleges of their day when they were Christian schools. If Christians could produce the top colleges in the early 1800s, surely we can do the same thing in the 2000s.

Second, consider the success of the homeschooling movement as an encouragement of what is possible. With no government funding and with limited experience, a group of basically untrained parents have produced what is widely recognized as the best form of K-12 academic education inside the space of a single generation. A movement to restore a Christian Ivy League could draw on an even wider slice of the Christian community. Christians who work together with a commitment to excellence can indeed accomplish great things.

Third, take a look at what is happening at Patrick Henry College. Even though I am its president, I hope you will allow me to talk about my own school for a moment—trying to be as objective as possible. Lest there be any misunderstanding, I hope that you, the reader, will understand that the same motivations that caused me to write this book were the reasons I started Patrick Henry College. I saw a need, and I believe it is inappropriate for Christians to say "here is a need" without being willing to do something to help *meet* the need. I am certainly not saying that PHC is the sole answer to any of the issues I have raised. I offer it here as an example and nothing more.

Even though PHC opened its doors in September 2000, it is already well on its way to becoming one of the top academic colleges in America. The median SAT score of PHC's incoming freshmen in the fall of 2004 is 1330.

U.S. News and World Report ranks college admission scores by identifying the middle fiftieth percentile. In other words, they present the scores of the twenty-fifth percentile to the seventy-fifth percentile of the entering class. Below are the scores for a few well-known secular and evangelical colleges. (To be able to compare apples to apples, I use the 2003 scores for all schools on this list.)

Harvard University	1400–1590
Yale University	1380–1580
Duke University	1330–1510
Vanderbilt University	1250–1430
University of Virginia	1230–1430
Wheaton College	1230–1410
Patrick Henry College	1230–1410
UCLA	1160–1410
Grove City College	1152–1378
Smith College	1150–1370
Pepperdine University	1090–1300
Hillsdale College	1090–1300*

Covenant College	1060–1320*
Baylor University	1070–1275
Calvin College	1060–1240
Cedarville University	1050–1260*
Bryan College	1030–1240
Biola University	1000–1220
Liberty University	870–1120

* Indicates school reported ACT scores that have been converted to SAT equivalent.

One way to make sense of the numbers is that fully half of the freshmen entering PHC in 2004 fall into the admissions band for Duke University—the fifth ranked university in the nation. Thirty-two percent of PHC entering freshmen scored above fourteen hundred, which would, based on scores only, place them within Harvard's reported middle admissions band.

The early academic success of Patrick Henry College, though, extends beyond entering scores. In our first four years, PHC won two national debate championships in the National Educational Debate Association, the college debate league that features courtroom or legislative speed of delivery. (There are two larger college leagues that feature speed debate, which sounds like auctioneering to most people.) We also have been a dominant team at the national Moot Court championships for the last few years. In 2003, PHC won as many trophies at that national tournament as all the other twenty-two colleges in the tournament combined. In the spring semester of 2004, PHC had more interns in the White House than any other college.

For those who are not familiar with the background of PHC, it is the only college in the nation in which 90 percent of the student body has been homeschooled. This distinctive has been the catalyst for attracting so many top students so quickly. That does not by any means imply that we are limited to homeschoolers. Top students attract other top students. We are getting students with higher and higher SAT scores from more states and a greater variety of educational backgrounds because of this factor.

I do not say this to claim that Patrick Henry is the only college in America that deserves the title of an aspiring member of the Christian Ivy League. I do not wish to make comparisons to other Christian colleges on either academics or fidelity to the Christian worldview.

Nevertheless, parents and donors should make inquiries into these areas. What is the college's view of the authority and inerrancy of Scripture? In particular, you should look at their view of evolution versus creation. Do they allow or teach theistic evolution? And what is their view of homosexual rights? Do they have gay student support organizations on campus?

Yes, I hope that Patrick Henry College will be considered a member of the Christian Ivy League. And yes, I hope that our students will be looked upon as having legitimacy in the eyes of the public. But I do not desire PHC to be the sole member of the Christian Ivy League. A number of schools should be striving for the top in a broad range of academic disciplines. We need leaders in all fields. I am particularly concerned about government, history, law, journalism, literature, and education, but we also need people at the top in science, medicine, engineering, business, and technology.

I would hope that several existing colleges are inspired to do an even better job of educating in a way that will enable them to gather a critical mass of elite students.

And I truly hope that many, many Christians who have the resources to support higher education in amounts large or small will see the strategic importance of the creation of top academic Christian institutions.

Patrick Henry College is an example that this is possible. We are not the only example. But, being frank, only a handful of Christian colleges attract students with high SAT scores. PHC is only five years old, and we consistently rank in the top few schools that profess an evangelical Christian worldview. And this doesn't even evaluate whether there are problems like theistic evolution in the other top-ranking evangelical schools. We need at least ten or twenty top schools in terms of academics that are absolutely unassailable in their faithfulness to the Word of God.

It is the goal of Patrick Henry College to start a law school before the end of this decade—hopefully by 2008. Currently, Regent University and Trinity International University are the only accredited law schools that, at least to my knowledge, have a strong evangelical, biblical worldview. Liberty University started a law school in September 2004, but, like any new school, it has to operate for awhile before gaining accreditation.

Just as there are several top secular law schools, we need several top Christian law schools. The goal should be to have at least one or two Christian law schools in the top twenty schools in the country within the next ten years. Yes, we need Christians who will practice law in all facets of the legal profession, but we also desperately need those who aim for the top. We need some who will clerk for the United States Supreme Court after law school. We need our people to work in the Solicitor General's office, which handles all of the federal government's cases in the Supreme Court. We need people who land legal jobs that place them in the position to become federal judges and law professors in the years ahead. If we put enough of our people into the "farm system," eventually some will start making it to the major leagues.

It will take around $50 million to launch a law school that can start strong enough to have a legitimate shot at penetrating the top rankings in a few years. That is a big number but not too big for God. And this brings me to my final and most important point.

Fourth, we need to remember that God is the author of any success that we will have.

Starting a college is a daunting task. And taking a college from the mid-level academically and moving it into the unquestioned ranks of the top schools in the nation is a huge challenge, but it *can* be done by the power and under the direction of God.

We have seen the hand of God at PHC in ways that leave no doubt of God's blessing and direction. We committed to starting a school with no debt and no government funding. The day we opened our doors, the *Washington Post* published a front-page story that quoted several experts who said the task we were starting was impossible—chiefly from a financial perspective. But five years later we still have never had to borrow money or take any government funds. God has defied the experts and supplied our needs.

We are not alone in this. God's provision is for His people, not a single college. I firmly believe that all who are committed to excellence and faithfulness will see God provide those things that are truly needed.

My views on commitment to excellence were impacted on my first trip to Hawaii in the 1980s. Vickie and I went to the island of Kauai and fell in love with its beauty. There was only one main road on the island, and we began to take note of the churches as we drove by looking for a place to go on Sunday.

I began to notice that many of the churches I would consider going to were not very high quality in terms of their buildings and maintenance. There was one church—the Latter Day Saints church—that had a beautiful building, impeccably maintained. It struck me that the outward quality of buildings is the first impression the world has about the way we view our relationship with God. If we invest time and resources to build quality and maintain what we build, it means that we place great value on what goes on inside. This does not mean that every church should be ornate or expensive. But it certainly should mean that our lawns are maintained and the paint looks fresh and the roof is not decomposed.

Why should Christians ever be second-rate on purpose? We should strive to be excellent in everything we do—for God's glory and as a reflection of *His* excellence. This includes the way we educate our young people.

Recently, I had a conversation on a soccer field with a woman I know from the community. She works for a branch of our local government. She came up to me and said, "I want to give you some unsolicited feedback on one of your students."

I have to tell you that I cringed inside because I know for a fact that her politics are much more liberal than my own.

She smiled broadly and began to exude praise on our students for his excellent work and great attitude when he interned in her office.

I found her comments to have important implications for the potential success of the Christian Ivy league. I have received other praise for our students. One person working in military intelligence sent an e-mail saying that the intern he had from PHC was the best he has ever had in sixteen years in supervising college interns. Since the military tends to be a bit more conservative, however, his comments were not as unexpected as the comments from the lady on the soccer field.

Her comments convinced me that excellence is appreciated across the political spectrum. It will open many doors. And I believe that just as the Left has moved our society in *its* direction through excellence, we can do the same in God's direction, only with greater spiritual power. The Bible says, "Do you see a man skilled in his work? He will serve before kings; he will not serve before obscure men" (Prov. 22:29).

God's ways work.

CHAPTER 9

There Is No "Homeschool Exception" to the Need for Hard Work

Success can breed complacency. Unfortunately, this attitude has already begun to creep into the homeschool movement.

No one should think that their children will have a top academic education merely because the instruction takes place in the family home. Without hard work, rigor, and persistence, homeschooling can produce a mediocre result.

I have been grading high school examinations in constitutional law for about six or seven years. I have graded thousands of papers written by homeschooled high schoolers.

About one-third of these papers were truly outstanding. About one-third were good or pretty good. About one-third needed a significant amount of work, particularly in the ability to write clear prose.

Of course, this is far better than the public school experience. There is no way that one-third of the public school students can write at the level I see among the top group of homeschoolers. I have shown sample exams (when I was riding on airplanes) to top professors who were amazed at the content and quality of the writing. In fact, one of the most highly regarded liberal professors of constitutional law in the nation was surprised at the quality of legal analysis and writing that I showed him on a recent flight.

Still, we have to face the fact that not every home-schooler writes at this level.

And not every bright student at Patrick Henry College succeeds. We have had students with high SATs do poorly. We have had students with more modest SATs (in the 1200s, for example) earn very high GPAs.

What is the difference? Hard work. Laziness never leads to success. As my dad used to say, an attitude of "I will" beats IQ every time.

Excellence will not come by accident. Nor will leadership skills come by osmosis.

Recall the statistics of high levels of civic activity among high school aged homeschool students offered in the first chapter. This is not going to happen in the next generation of homeschoolers unless something is done to make it happen.

The first generation of homeschoolers are now eighteen to thirty years old. They went through the season of home-school persecution that we all faced in the 1980s and early 1990s.

In the 1980s, the children of homeschoolers were acutely aware of the legal and political difficulties faced by their families. They went with their parents to court hearings. They were in the state capitols lobbying for homeschooling freedom. They worked in campaigns. They were activists because their parents were activists. They all *had* to be activists for basic survival.

While there are still plenty of legal troubles out there, the climate in general is much, much better. The children of homeschoolers today are not automatically going to get the same level of intense exposure to the political process as was generally available in the 1980s. Without direct involvement in politics, the next wave of homeschoolers may prove to be as indifferent to the future of our nation as other young people.

This does not mean that we are doomed as home-schoolers to be "one-hit wonders." We can achieve the same kind of results as the first generation *if we take deliberate steps of action* to give our children exposure to the real world of politics.

If your son or daughter gets involved in a political campaign to help a great candidate try to win public office, your child will be inspired to be an active citizen for his or her entire life. A student who works on a ballot initiative will see the same kind of lifelong results.

If you tell your teenagers to take your church directory and go to the county voter registration office to see who is not registered to vote, you will have *surprised* teens when they find that about half are not registered (if your church is typical). Then, if you encourage your teens to pick up voter registration forms, talk with those who are not registered, and offer them an opportunity to register on the spot, you will have *involved* teens. And if you encourage your teens to follow up with those they helped register to make sure they actually vote, you will have *motivated* teens who realize that even if they are not eighteen, they can effectively vote multiple times in an election by getting unregistered voters to the polls.

Home School Legal Defense Association has launched a long-term project to make sure that the homeschool teens of the future have real-life opportunities to work on issues and campaigns that really matter. Learning about how a bill becomes law from a textbook is one of the most boring things imaginable. But if you are working on a bill that you care about, you want to know how a bill becomes a law so that you can win and make a difference.

Our program is called Generation Joshua. It will have both civics education and hands-on opportunity. Contact HSLDA on the Web to get more information (www.genera tionjoshua.org or www.hslda.org).

If we work hard to achieve academic excellence and if we give our students the kind of hands-on experience that provides lifelong motivation, we will continue to produce a disproportionate number of young people who are equipped to be leaders.

CHAPTER 10

The Joshua Generation Needs Wisdom, Not Mere Knowledge

A seductive power works in any form of achievement. Our human pride can lead us into foolishness even in the midst of our excellence.

Without the desire to succeed, we accomplish little. Those who are content to be mediocre are rarely tempted by pride, but they rarely achieve anything worthwhile. The desire to succeed needs to be tempered by a healthy understanding of who God is and who each of us is before Him.

Specifically, the desire for knowledge cannot be the pinnacle of our educational desires. Rather, we should strive for wisdom—not humanly defined wisdom but that form of wisdom *God* encourages us to achieve.

In my opinion, the failure of Harvard and Yale to stay on a godly course came from their elevation of human knowledge over and above godly wisdom.

Let's look at several key passages of Scripture that give us the keys to wisdom for leaders.

Leaders Need to Have the Wisdom to Be the First to Obey God

Psalm 2:10–12 is addressed to kings and rulers of the earth—that is, leaders:

> Therefore, you kings, be wise;
> be warned, you rulers of the earth.
> Serve the LORD with fear
> and rejoice with trembling.
> Kiss the Son, lest he be angry
> and you be destroyed in your way,
> for his wrath can flare up in a moment.
> Blessed are all who take refuge in him.

God warns leaders to serve Him with fear and trembling. There is a tendency among rulers to think that they are above the fray, that they are so special that God's rules do not apply to them because they bear the extra burdens of leadership.

God does not buy that kind of reasoning. Leaders need to be the *first* to serve the Lord with fear, not the last. We are the most harshly judged, not those who will receive special leniency. Jesus said, "From everyone who has been given much, much will be required; and to whom they entrusted much, of him they will ask all the more" (Luke 12:48 NASB). And in the book of James, we read, "Not many of you should presume to be teachers, my brothers, because you know that we who teach will be judged more strictly" (James 3:1).

Wise Leaders Are Humble

Proverbs 15:33 instructs, "The fear of the LORD teaches a man wisdom, and humility comes before honor."

Leaders fill positions of honor and trust. There is nothing inherently wrong with this. However, a wise person is not motivated by a self-serving, prideful attitude. Each of us must start with an attitude of humility if God is to be the source of our position of honor.

The best way to learn humility is to serve others with a sincere heart. Humility is not saying bad things about your abilities or talents. Saying, "Oh, I am no good" is drawing attention to yourself. In fact, it is a backwards way of expressing pride in your humility. True humility is found in using your talents and your time to help other people achieve their goals.

A mother is the world's best example of humility. She sacrifices her time and energy—indeed, her very life—for the good of her children. She wants them to succeed.

She doesn't need to refuse their thanks for her work. She doesn't need to engage in self-deprecating talk that cries out, "I am but a worm." No, she simply works hard to meet the needs of her children and basks in their success. In fact, their success *is* her success in many ways.

The selflessness of a mother is the path to true honor.

Wisdom Comes from Small Acts of Faithfulness

Daniel is a premier example of a godly person who rose to a position of leadership through his wisdom and understanding. Daniel 1:19–20 records:

> The king talked with them, and he found none
> equal to Daniel, Hananiah, Mishael and Azariah; so
> they entered the king's service. In every matter of
> wisdom and understanding about which the king
> questioned them, he found them ten times better

than all the magicians and enchanters in his whole kingdom.

What did Daniel do to make him so wise? He ate vegetables. (This is not my subtle way of advocating vegetarianism. I eat lots of meat and few vegetables.) Daniel ate vegetables out of obedience to God because the only other available diet would have violated his convictions about God's dietary requirements. In other words Daniel was faithful in a little thing, and God blessed him abundantly.

This is a general principle of God's ways. Matthew 25:21 tells us God's reply to the servant who had been faithful with the talents given him: "His master replied, 'Well done, good and faithful servant! You have been faithful with a few things; I will put you in charge of many things. Come and share your master's happiness!'"

This principle is one of the most important lessons in my own life.

A couple of months after starting law school, I felt a strong sense of conviction one Sunday during church. I have no idea what the message was about, but the thoughts running through my mind were, *Everyone in your classes knows that you are a constitutional hotshot and a conservative. When are you going to tell anyone that you are a Christian?*

I was pierced to the quick and knew that if I wanted to remain right with God, I needed to respond right away. The next day at school, I took a single sheet of yellow paper off my legal tablet and wrote: "Anyone interested in starting a law students' Bible study, contact Mike Farris." I gave my phone number. Then I posted it on the announcement board.

The word spread rapidly through the law school, and some teasing was sent my way but nothing that would remotely count as persecution.

Some time later I called a local attorney named Ray Eberle whom I had never met but who was widely reported to be a strong Christian. I introduced myself and asked him if he would like to speak to our law students Bible study.

He said, "Yeah, I have heard about your study. I'll come. And would you like a job?"

I said yes. And that was it. That was my entire job interview.

One day I was parking my car across the street from the Spokane Opera House in the lot where I regularly parked for work. One of my friends from law school was walking on the other side of the street next to the Opera House. He yelled out to me, "Hey, Farris! They are opening up a tavern in the Opera House, and we can go get drunk together . . . ha ha ha." He knew that I didn't drink.

I went over to take a look. It turned out that there were two liquor licenses being pursued in the beautiful city park that had been a part of the Spokane World's Fair a few years earlier. One was to be a part-time liquor outlet in the Opera House, the other a full-time tavern in the middle of the park as a part of a food service area.

It struck me as the wrong thing to do. Why did we need alcohol in a city park dedicated to kids and families?

I formed a group that I called Citizens Opposed to Opera House Liquor, which I abbreviated as COOL. We held press conferences, ran a petition drive, and notified the state liquor control board that the project was in a city park. The press never asked me how many people were members of COOL. Actually there were just two: an eighty-year-old lady who had been a member of the Women's Christian Temperance Union and me. We were both citizens. And we were opposed to liquor in the Opera House.

The state liquor control board stopped the full-time tavern in the park and let the Opera House facility proceed.

As a result of all the surrounding publicity, I was invited to join a statewide pro-family organization called The Umbrella Group. After I joined that group, feminists succeeded in getting Congress to give them another three years to ratify the Equal Rights Amendment after the original seven years expired. Dottie Roberts, one of the founders of The Umbrella Group called me and told me that the ERA extension had passed.

"Is this constitutional?" she asked me.

I was two years out of law school and still felt like I was a constitutional whiz kid. (I had a lot to learn.) But I answered her with great confidence, "It is utterly unconstitutional."

"Then what are you going to do about it?" she demanded. You didn't tell Dottie that something was wrong unless you were willing to join the fight.

I ended up representing three Washington State legislators in the first lawsuit to challenge that extension. (Our challenge was later consolidated with another case, and we proceeded ahead as a team.)

While working on that case, I called Beverly LaHaye to see if she would do a fund-raising rally for our lawsuit. She was just starting Concerned Women for America at the time. She graciously agreed.

Shortly after that I organized another rally where Tim LaHaye was the featured speaker.

Not long after that, Tim and Beverly called me and offered me a job with Concerned Women for America. I accepted.

At a television taping for the LaHayes I was introduced to the idea of homeschooling. As a result of that, I started Home School Legal Defense Association.

And the story can keep on going and going. Running for Lieutenant Governor. Starting Patrick Henry College. And more.

I can trace every single significant career move in my entire life back to that yellow piece of paper where I started the law students' Bible study. It was a little thing. I don't know why I was so scared to tell anyone that I was a Christian. I was foolish. All I did was correct a season of cowardly foolishness.

God chose to bless my small act of obedience in ways that are dramatically out of proportion to what I did. One small act of obedience led to a bigger opportunity. While I cannot claim any status as a super-Christian, I *can* say that continued small acts of obedience have led to greater and greater career opportunities. I have been faithful in a few things. God has blessed me with opportunities that are greatly beyond anything I deserve.

The path to leadership requires small acts of obedience. From those acts God gives wisdom and understanding. When we do these things, we may look great compared to those around us, but it is not really about us anyway; it is God-given wisdom that really wows people today just as Daniel wowed the king of Babylon.

To the degree I am successful, it is not because I am "so smart" or because I have seven years of college. It is because God has blessed small acts of obedience.

I would not want anyone to believe that academic excellence is not important as a result of that story. I won the Moot Court championship in law school, made the law review, and graduated with honors near the top of my class. Those acts of preparation were helpful, perhaps necessary. But I know enough about God that He blesses those who are both prepared and faithful. Neither by itself is sufficient.

Failing to be prepared—that is, not being the best you can be before God—is, in reality, a lack of faithfulness. We should be good stewards of the talents and opportunities God gives us.

Christian leaders are needed. You can be smart. You can go to a great school and do well. But if you fail to be faithful, you will be disqualified from Christian leadership.

God's plan will not be thwarted by any individual's lack of faithfulness. I truly believe that He wants to bless this nation in the next generation and that there are exciting things in store for those who are prepared and faithful. If you are disqualified because of repeated personal moral failings, God's plan will succeed, but it will not include you.

The Joshua Generation can turn America back to the spirit of the founding fathers and be remembered as a truly pivotal generation in our nation's history. If you want to be a part of it, you can. Work hard. Be excellent. Be faithful. Be humble. Pursue wisdom.

May the God of our Fathers grant us a renewed nation through the blessings that come when a righteous remnant dedicates itself to following God in every way.

Concluding Thoughts

Immanuel Kant is one of the most significant philosophers of the last three centuries. Kant argues that the basic rules of morality are rational and that all men in all cultures can logically deduce these principles. As Ravi Zacharias points out in his book *Can Man Live without God?* "Kant does not deny that God has given us some commands. He just denies the need for that revelation since reason alone, he contends, impels us to what is right."[1]

Today's secular academics consider themselves to be the rightful descendents of the philosophy of Immanuel Kant. However, they are not the only ones who claim to walk in the footsteps of Kant. As Zacharias points out: "both democracies and totalitarian regimes lay claim to Kant's philosophy as the groundwork for their social theories."[2]

The sad reality is that it is not only the secular west and totalitarian regimes who embrace the philosophy of Immanuel Kant. As disclosed by the research of The Barna Group, discussed in the early chapters, the vast majority of born-again Christian teenagers think more like Immanuel Kant than the apostle Paul. By believing that morality is situational and personal rather than God-given and absolute, Christian young people have embraced the key element of a foreign antitheistic philosophy.

When the education we offer these young people leaves God out of the equation, no other result is possible. Removing God as the source of morality makes amorality and situational ethics are the inevitable results.

Unfortunately, not just young people are affected by the Kantian approach that leaves God out. I have been deeply involved in the battle over same-sex marriage. Far too many conservatives are taking the position that while they oppose same-sex marriage, they will allow the states to create civil unions for homosexuals. This leads to the question: what are the differences between civil unions and marriage? The answer is: civil unions grant 100 percent of the legal rights of marriage. A license from the government is required to enter the union. A government order similar to a divorce decree is required to dissolve the civil union. And, again, all the rights of marriage are given to civil union couples. The only difference is the word *marriage*.

The arguments that we attempt to make against same-sex marriage are severely diminished when we concede the option of civil unions. How can we say it is morally wrong? How can we argue the sanctity of marriage when we are willing to bless these living arrangements by using another name?

Christians have taken to arguing against same-sex marriage purely on the basis of social science research.

Here is the problem. When we enter the territory of social science research and leave God out of our arguments, we have conceded our most essential weapon in battle— God's standard of truth. Social science that operates in

Kantian fashion will inevitably prove itself to favor the moral conclusions that are contrary to the moral standards of God. When Christians leave God out, we cannot possibly win, because no one can know the truth apart from God.

Christian homeschooling has demonstrated that it is still possible today to provide an education that is both academically excellent and faithful to the principles of God. Although it is still early, there is every reason to believe that these young people as adults can have a tremendous impact on our society for good if they are trained to think not according to the philosophy of Immanuel Kant but according to the truth of "Immanuel, God with us."

Notes

Chapter 1

1. *Strengths of Their Own—Home Schoolers Across America* (Salem, Ore.: National Home Education Research Institute, 1997).
2. *Baptist News*, 12 June 2002.
3. *The Barna Update*, 24 September 2003.
4. *The Barna Update*, 12 February 2002.
5. For more information go to http://rmromania.org.

Chapter 2

1. *Grutter v. Bollinger*, 539 U.S. 332.
2. I attended Whitman College, an elite small liberal arts college for my freshman and sophomore years. It is a secular school. I graduated from a state college, now called Western Washington University. I also graduated from Gonzaga University School of Law, a Jesuit college. Gonzaga is secular despite its Jesuit connection. I received not one minute of Christian or Catholic education in my three years there. And the more objective proof is Gonzaga's current practices. The law school has banned the Christian Legal Society from the campus because it requires Christian leadership. The law school has a gay and lesbian student club that is fully sanctioned. Any claim to being a Christian college is absolutely forfeited under such circumstances.

Chapter 3

1. Howard Zinn, *A People's History of the United States* (New York: Harper & Row, 1980), 59.
2. Ibid., 65.
3. Ibid., 58.
4. Ibid., 99.
5. Ibid.
6. Ibid., 394; Zinn adds later in the same paragraph that capitalism "had brought depression and crisis—the system of waste, of inequality, of concern for profit over human need."
7. Ibid., 416.
8. For example, ibid., 13–14 say, "When the Pilgrims came to New England they too were coming not to vacant land but to territory inhabited by tribes of Indians. The governor of the Massachusetts Bay Colony, John Winthrop, created the excuse to take Indian land by declaring the area legally a 'vacuum.' . . . The Puritans also appealed to the Bible, Psalms 2:8: 'Ask of me, and I shall give thee, the heathen for thine inheritance, and the uttermost parts of the earth for thy possession.' And to justify their use of force to take the land, they cited Romans 13:2: 'Whosoever therefore resisteth the power, resisteth the ordinance of God: and they that resist shall receive themselves damnation.'" Zinn also writes on pages 106–107: "No wonder that Puritan New England carried over this subjection of women. At a trial of a woman for daring to complain about the work a carpenter had done for her, one of the powerful church fathers of Boston, the Reverend John Cotton, said: 'that the husband should obey the wife, and not the wife the husband, that is a false principle. For God hath put another law upon women: wives be subject to your husbands in all things.'"
9. Ibid., 504.
10. Ibid., 113, 499.
11. Ibid., 20.

12. Alexis de Tocqueville, *Democracy in America*, vol. 2 (New York: Vintage Classics, 1990), 115, as quoted in Daniel J. Flynn, *Why the Left Hates America: Exposing the Lies That Have Obscured Our Nation's Greatness* (New York: Forum Prima, 2002), 116.

13. To emphasize the point, a few other schools include University of Houston ("U.S. from 1877 to the Present"), Syracuse University ("Differences in Photographic Histories"), Case Western University ("Introduction to American History"), Victor Valley College ("U.S. History from 1870"), Hartnell College (U.S. History, part II), University of Central Florida ("U.S. History since 1877"), Cal State University at Pomona ("U.S. History from 1865 to the Present"), Gavilan College ("History 1: U.S. History to 1876"), Dartmouth College ("English 5: Militarism, Pacifism, and Consent"), Modesto Junior College ("History of The United States, 1865–2003 Reconstruction through the Modern Era"), Palo Alto College ("U.S. History 1302"), Southwestern University ("Economic History of the United States"), University of Louisiana at Lafayette ("American Literature before 1865"), Eastern Kentucky University ("History of the United States to 1877"), Cal State San Marcos ("United States History from 1865"), Cleveland State University ("United States History: Discovering Freedom in America"), Cal State Humboldt (History 111), and Cal State Monterey Bay ("Social and Political Histories of the United States").

14. "Ivory tower," *The American Heritage Dictionary of the English Language*, 4th ed. (Boston: Houghton Mifflin, 2000).

15. "About S. Weddington," The Weddington Center: The Center for Leadership, at http://www.theweddington center.com/leadershipbio.html.

16. Rick Perlstein, "Moment of Decision," *University of Chicago Magazine*, vol. 95, no. 1, August 2003, at http://maga zine.uchicago.edu/0308/features/index3.shtml.

17. Keppler Associates Inc, "Howard Zinn Biography," http://www.kepplerassociates.com/speakers/zinnhoward.asp?1.

18. The Department of History and Political Science, "Howard Zinn to Speak at Manchester on September 29, 2004," Manchester College, http://www.manchester.edu/Academics/Departments/HPS/news1.htm.

19. Ibid.

20. Howard Zinn, "Tennis on the Titanic," ZNet Daily Commentaries, http://www.zmag.org/sustainers/content/2000-12/16zinn.htm; Zinn's commentary also gives us a flavor of the kind of policies he would prefer: the reduction of prisons and the military and an end to "corporate control of the economy."

21. Howard Zinn, quoted in David Barsamian, "The Future of History, Part I: An Interview with Howard Zinn," ZMag Online, http://www.zmag.org/zmag/articles/mar99 barzinn.htm.

22. Ibid.

23. Shirley Chisholm, excerpt from *Unbought and Unbossed* in *In Praise of Our Teachers: A Multicultural Tribute to Those Who Inspired Us*, ed. Gloria Wade Gayles (Boston: Beacon Press, 2003), 30.

24. Angela Davis, excerpt from *Angela Davis: An Autobiography*, in ibid., 118–19.

25. Marian Wright Edelman, excerpt from *Lanterns: A Memoir of Mentors*, in ibid., 111–13.

26. Ibid.

27. "What Is Accuracy in Academia?" Accuracy in Academia, at http://www.academia.org/about.html.

28. Students for Academic Freedom, at http://www.stu dentsforacademicfreedom.org.

29. Congress, House, H.Con.Res.318, 108th Cong., 1st sess.; text at http://thomas.loc.gov/cgi-bin/bdquery/z?d108:HC00318:@@@L&summ2=m&.

30. Congress, Senate, Committee on Health, Education, Labor, & Pensions, *Is Intellectual Diversity an Endangered*

Species on America's College Campuses?, 108th Cong., 1st sess., 29 October 2003.

31. Course catalog at http://www.harvard.edu.

32. Christopher Phelps, Ohio State University, "Why We Shouldn't Call It War," *The Chronicle of Higher Education* 48, no. 5 (28 September 2001): B11; Catherine Lutz, University of North Carolina at Chapel Hill, "Our Legacy of War," *The Chronicle of Higher Education* 48, no. 5 (28 September 2001): B14.

33. Malcolm A. Kline, "The Academic XXXstablishment," *Campus Report Online*, 18 June 2004, at http://www.campus reportonline.net/main/articles.php?id=117; "College Gets an F for X-Rated Conferences," *Education Reporter*, January 1998, at http://www.eagleforum.org/educate/1998/jan98/college.html.

34. Robert Brandon, quoted in "Debating Party Purity in Faculty Population," *Duke Magazine*, May/June 2004, at http://www.dukemagzine.duke.edu/dukemag/issues/050604/depgaz.html.

35. "The Shame of America's One-Party Campuses," *American Enterprise*, September 2002, 18.

36. Ibid., 19–25, citing research by TAE and the Center for the Study of Popular Culture.

37. Quoted in Richard Leiby, "The Reliable Source," *Washington Post*, 25 May 2004, C03.

38. Ibid.

39. David Horowitz, "Executive Summary: Study of Bias in the Selection of Commencement Speakers at 32 Elite Colleges and Universities," 2003, at http://www.studentsforacade micfreedom.org/reports/liberalbias.html.

40. Ibid.

41. Robert Stacy McCain, "Poll Confirms Ivy League Liberal Tilt," *The Washington Times*, 15 January 2002, A6.

42. Ibid.

43. Ibid.

44. As reported by Frank Luntz, "Inside the Mind of an Ivy League Professor," *FrontPageMagazine.com*, 30 August 2002, at http://www.frontpagemag.com/Articles/ReadArticle.asp?ID=2642.

45. Ibid.

46. Ibid.

47. Duncan Kennedy, "First Year Law Teaching as Political Action," *Law & Social Problems* 1, no. 47 (1980): 55.

48. Alan Dershowitz, "Defining Academic Freedom," *Harvard Crimson*, 30 June 1995, at http://www.thecrimson.com/printerfriendly.aspx?ref=238084.

49. Shapiro, 85, quoting from "Globalization and Its Discontents," *TIME Europe Web Exclusive*, 30 January 2000.

50. Ibid., quoting from David F. Salisbury, "Computer Pioneer Discusses Atheism, Artificial Intelligence," *Stanford Report Online*, 17 March 1999.

51. "Report: Ethics, Enron, and American Higher Education: An NAS/Zogby Poll of College Seniors," National Association of Scholars, July 2002, at http://www.nas.org/reports/zogethics_poll/zogby_ethics_report.htm.

52. Ibid.

53. Ibid.

54. Ron Puhek, *Mind, Soul, and Spirit: An Inquiry into the Spiritual Derailments of Modern Life* (n.p.: Out Your Backdoor, 1998), text available at http://www.glpbooks.com/oyb/Fifth way/Spirittext.htm.

55. Elizabeth Kiss in an interview by Gary Pavela, "Teaching Character in College," available at http://www.jpo.umd.edu/ethical/elizkiss.html.

56. Quotations from "What's the Story?" and "Reviews & Awards," at http://www.daddyandpapa.com.

57. See Robinson's Stanford faculty home page at http://history.stanford.edu/faculty/robinson.

58. Diane Manuel, "Getting Personal: An Intellectual Historian 'Dives for the Genitals,'" *Stanford Magazine*, at

http://www.stanfordalumni.org/news/magazine/1999/julaug/shelf_life/author_author.html.

59. Ibid.

60. "Yale College Programs of Study," Yale University, available at http://www.yale.edu/yalecollege/publications/ycps/chapter_iv/index.html.

61. Ibid.

62. Anne D. Neal and Jerry L. Martin, page 11 of Appendix C, *Restoring America's Legacy*, A Report by the American Council of Trustees and Alumni (Washington, D.C.: ACTA, September 2002).

63. "About Calvin College: Mission & Promise," Calvin College Web site, at http://www.calvin.edu/about.

64. "Discussion Group for Gay and Lesbian Students: Group Introduction," Calvin College Web site, at http://www.calvin.edu/admin/broene/galsac/group_intro.htm.

65. Julianne Smith, "Gay Debate II Focuses on Showing Real People," *Calvin College Chimes*, 12 March 1999, at http://clubs.calvin.edu/chimes/990312/news/news2.html.

66. Peggy Cooper Davis, "Progressive Constitutionalism and the People: Neglected Stories and Progressive Constitutionalism," *Widener Law Symposium,* Spring 1999.

67. Ibid.

68. Peggy Cooper Davis, "Neglected Stories and the Lawfulness of *Roe v. Wade*," *Harvard Civil Rights-Civil Liberties Law Review,* Spring 1993.

69. "The Missing Middle: Working Families and the Future of American Social Policy," The Century Foundation Event Summary, 12 April 2000, at http://www.tcf.org/Events/04-12-00/summary.pdf.

70. See Hochschild's Harvard faculty home page at http://www.gov.harvard.edu/Faculty/Bios/Hochschild.htm.

71. Ibid.

72. Jennifer Hochschild, "Bush's First Six Months: Trouble in the Tent," *Newsday*, 12 August 2001, B04; This article was

reprinted as a "Featured View" by Common Dreams, which describes itself as "a national nonprofit citizens' organization working to bring progressive Americans together to promote progressive visions for America's future" (http://www.common dreams.org).

73. Quoted in Adam P. Schneider, "Zinn Speaks Out against Iraq Occupation, Summers," *The Harvard Crimson*, 5 December 2003, at http://www.thecrimson.com/article .aspx?ref=356645.

74. Remarks by Anne Neal, Hearing by Senate Committee on Health, Education, Labor, & Pensions, *Is Intellectual Diversity an Endangered Species on America's College Campuses?*, 108th Cong., 1st sess., 29 October 2003, quoting "Criticism Becomes Dogmatism," *Columbia Spectator*, 27 March 2003, at http://www.columbiaspectator.com/vnews/dis play.v/ART/2003/03/27/3e82ee188475e.

75. Ibid.

76. Jerry L. Martin and Anne D. Neal, *Defending Civilization: How Our Universities Are Failing America and What Can Be Done about It*, A Project of the Defense of Civilization Fund and the American Council of Trustees and Alumni, February 2002, 20, quoting William J. Bennett, "Maddening Deeds at U.S. Universities," *Boston Globe*, 4 November 2001.

77. Daniel J. Flynn, Why the Left Hates America: Exposing the Lies That Have Obscured Our Nation's Greatness (New York: Prima Lifestyles, a division of Random House, 2002), chapter 2, "The Roots of Anti-Americanism."

78. Ibid., 11.

79. Ibid., 18, quoting Tony Francetic, "University May Be Infringing on Students' Rights," *Central Michigan Life*, 10 October 2001, 1.

80. James Taranto, "Their Eyes Are Brown," from the Best of the Web Today, Opinion Journal, *Wall Street Journal*, 11 October 2001, at http://www.opinionjournal.com/best/ ?id=95001303.

81. Ibid.

82. Martin and Neal, 14, quoting "Code Red Herring," *Washington Bulletin*: National Review's Internet Update for 1 October 2001.

83. Ibid., 25, quoting the Foundation for Individual Rights in Education Web site, at http://www.thefire.org.

84. Flynn, 25-26, quoting Christopher Chow, "Tufts 'Non-Violence' Activists Attack Patriotic Student," *Campus Report*, November 2001, 7.

85. Ibid.

86. Ibid., 20.

87. Quoted in "University Community Tries to Understand, Cope with Tragedy," Princeton Web Announcement, at https://www.princeton.edu/webannouncecgi/NP_get_news_arti cle_by_id.pl?archived=Y&id=12084.

88. Ibid.

89. Ibid., 26, quoting Anemona Hartocollis, "CUNY Chief Repudiates Forum Remarks," *New York Times*, 4 October 2001.

90. Flynn, 167.

Chapter 4

1. 478 U.S. 186.

2. 539 U.S. 558.

3. Historians cannot seem to agree who was the original author of this saying. Various sources credit John Seeley, E. A. Freeman, and Lord Acton, to name a few.

4. Alexander Fraser Tytler, *Universal History: From the Creation of the World to the Beginning of the Eighteenth Century*, vol. 1 (Boston: Hilliard, Gray, and Company, 1837), 464.

5. Ibid.

6. M. Stanton Evans, *The Theme Is Freedom: Religion, Politics, and the American Tradition* (Washington, D.C.: Regnery Publishing, Inc., 1994), 15–16.

7. See, for example, the simply glowing praise of Emma Goldman on a Web site maintained on the University of California (Berkeley) Web page. http://sunsite.berke ley.edu/Goldman. Not only does Goldman receive profuse verbal praise, but Web visitors are also encouraged to purchase "Emmarabilia" to further the work of preserving her legacy.

8. Howard Zinn, "Unsung Heroes," *The Progressive Magazine*, June 2000, at http://www.progressive.org/zinn 0600.htm.

9. See, for instance, John Demos, "Using Self, Using History," *The Journal of American History* 89, no. 1, June 2002, 37. He is discussed later in this chapter.

10. Nancy Cott, "Testimony of Nancy F. Cott, Jonathan Trumbull Professor of American History, Harvard University In Support of H.3677 (Civil Marriage); H.1149, S.935, and S.1045 (Civil Unions)," 23 October 2003, at http:// www.glad.org/GLAD_Cases/Nancy_Cott_testimony.pdf.

11. Francis Schaeffer, *The Church at the End of the Twentieth Century* (1970), *The Complete Works of Francis A Schaeffer: A Christian Worldview, A Christian View of the Church*, 2nd ed. (Westchester, Ill.: Crossway Books, 1982), 11.

12. "Hillary and Julie Goodridge, et al. v. Department of Public Health: Plaintiffs' Filings," Gay & Lesbian Advocates and Defenders, at http://www.glad.org/marriage/goodridge_ amici.shtml.

13. SJC–08860.

14. Brief posted on Lambda Legal's site at http://www.lamb dalegal.org/cgi-bin/iowa/documents/record?record=1190.

15. "George Chauncey," University of Chicago History Department Faculty Listings, at http://history.uchicago.edu/ faculty/chauncey.html.

16. Rick Perlstein, "Moment of Decision," *University of Chicago Magazine*, August 2003, at http://magazine.uchi cago.edu/0308/features/index.shtml.

17. Ibid.

18. These were generally not sponsored by fringe groups, either. For example, the sponsors listed for the University of Illinois appearance include the "Office of the Chancellor; Office of the Provost and Vice Chancellor for Academic Affairs; Office of the Vice Chancellor for Research and the Graduate College; Office of the Vice Chancellor for Student Affairs; The Council of Deans; The Center for Advanced Study; George A. Miller Endowment; George A. Miller Committee; Peggy Harris Memorial Fund; Office of Affirmative Action; School of Art and Design; Department of Anthropology; Department of English; Department for Germanic Languages and Literatures; Department of History; Department of Journalism; Department of Philosophy; Department of Political Science; Department of Psychology; Department of Spanish, Italian, and Portuguese; Afro-American Studies and Research Program; Campus Honors Program; Humanities Council/LAS; Medical Humanities Program; Office of Lesbian, Gay, Bisexual and Transgender Concerns; Office of Minority Student Affairs; Program for the Study of Cultural Values and Ethics; WILL-AM Radio; Unit for Criticism and Interpretive Theory; Women's Studies Program; McKinley Presbyterian Foundation."

19. The announcement at http://www.cla.umn.edu/cafs/co loquium.html says, "The Feminist Studies Colloquium is presented by the Department of Women's Studies and the Center for Advanced Feminist Studies, with the generous cosponsorship of the Humanities Institute, the College of Liberal Arts and the Interdisciplinary Center for the Study of Global Change." Center for Advanced Feminist Studies? Interdisciplinary Center for the Study of Global Change? No wonder they like him.

20. "Sexual Orientations and American Culture" at Fullerton has six required readings: Martin Bauml Duberman's *Hidden from History: Exploring the Gay and Lesbian Past*, George Chauncey's *Gay New York: Gender, Urban Culture, and the Making of the Gay Male World, 1890-1940*, Lillian

Faderman's *Odd Girls and Twilight Lovers: A History of Lesbian Life in Twentieth-Century America*, Ritch C. Savin-Williams's ". . . *And Then I Became Gay*": *Young Men's Stories*, Lindsey Elder's *Early Embraces: True-Life Stories of Women Describing Their First Lesbian Experience*, and John D'Emilio and Estelle B. Freedman's "The Reproductive Matrix, 1600–1800."

21. Ibid.

22. Beth Portier, "Pioneering Women's Historian Joins FAS, Schlesinger," *Harvard Gazette*, 17 October 2002, at http://www.news.harvard.edu/gazette/2002/10.17/03-cott.html.

23. Ibid.

24. Nancy Cott, *Public Vows: A History of Marriage and the Nation* (Cambridge, Mass.: Harvard University Press, 2000), 20–21.

25. Ibid., 22.

26. Ibid., 226.

27. Ibid., 216.

28. Nancy Cott, "Testimony of Nancy F. Cott, Jonathan Trumbull Professor of American History, Harvard University in Support of H.3677 (Civil Marriage); H.1149, S.935, and S.1045 (Civil Unions)," GLAD Marriage Testimonies, at http://www.glad.org/GLAD_Cases/testimony_10_23_03.shtml.

29. George Chauncey, "The Ridicule of Gay and Lesbian Studies Threatens All Academic Inquiry," *Chronicle of Higher Education* 44, no. 43 (1998): A40.

30. Thomas Bartlett, "The Most Hated Professor in America," *The Chronicle of Higher Education* online, 18 April 2003, at http://chronicle.com/free/v49/i32/32a05601.htm.

31. Ibid.

32. Ibid.; "The Faculty: Department of Anthropology," Columbia University, at http://www.columbia.edu/cu/anthropology.html.

33. Glenda Gilmore, "What Glenda Gilmore Really Said," History News Network, 14 April 2003, at http://hnn.us/articles/1395.html.

34. Ibid.

35. "Founding Statement," Historians Against the War, at http://historiansagainstwar.org/press03jan03.html.

36. "Statement on the U.S. Occupation of Iraq," Historians Against the War, at http://historiansagainstwar.org/press 21sept03.html.

37. Anne Winkler-Morey, "Teach-In: University of Minnesota," Historians Against the War, at http://historians againstwar.org/teachin/umn.html.

38. Ibid; "Our Mission," Women Against Military Madness, at http://www.worldwidewamm.org.

39. Gilberto Reyes Jr., "U.S. Hispanics Ethically Compelled to Oppose War," Historians Against the War, Virtual Movement Archive, at http://historiansagainstwar.org/re yes.html.

40. Ibid.

41. Dear Colleague letter, "Civil Liberties and Academic Freedom," Historians Against the War, at http://www.histori ansagainstwar.org/freedom/genova.html.

42. See Legal Community Against Violence, at http:// www.lcav.org/library/featured_topics/second_amendment/char lton_heston_nytsad.asp.

43. Ibid.

44. Carl T. Bogus, "The History and Politics of the Second Amendment Scholarship: A Primer," Symposium on the Second Amendment, *Chicago-Kent Law Review* 76, no. 1 (2000): 5.

45. Letter to Charlton Heston; see sponsor's Web site at http://www.firearmslawcenter.org/library/featured_topics/sec ond_amendment/An_Open_Letter_to_the_NRA.pdf.

46. Jack Rakove, quoted in Amy L. Kovac, "Taking Aim— NRA, scholars clash over Second Amendment," *The Stanford Daily*, 30 March 2000, at http://daily.stanford.edu/ tempo?page=content&id=1875&repository=0001_article.

47. Ibid.

48. Jack Rakove, *Original Meanings: Politics and Ideas in the Making of the Constitution* (New York: Vintage Books, 1996), xv.

49. Anuj Gupta, "History Profs Assail House—Scholars Criticize Attack on 'Constitutional Order,'" *The Stanford Daily*, 3 November 1998, at http://daily.stanford.edu/daily/servlet/tempo?page=content&id=4577&repository=0001_article.

50. Ibid., quoting Jack Rakove.

51. "Historians in Defense of the Liberal Conspiracy," *The American Enterprise*, vol. 10, no. 1, January/February 1999, 10.

52. Quoted in Michael Barone, "Forgetting the Founding Fathers," *Catholic Exchange*, at http://www.catholic exchange.com/vm/index.asp?art_id=24072&vm_id=1&action_type=get_results&quiz_id=486&typeid=1&answer=1521&sub mit1=submit.

53. Jon Butler, "Religion and the American Founding," "Stories from the Revolution, The American Revolution: Lighting Freedom's Flame," at http://www.nps.gov/revwar/about_the_revolution/religion.html.

54. Ibid.

55. Charles F. James, *Documentary History of the Struggle for Religious Liberty in Virginia* (Lynchburg, VA: J.P. Bell Company, 1900; reprint, New York: Da Capo Press, 1971), 66; Daniel L. Dreisbach, "Church-State Debate in the Virginia Legislature: From the Declaration of Rights to the Statue for Establishing Religious Freedom," in Garrett Ward Sheldon and Daniel L. Dreisbach, *Religion and Political Culture in Jefferson's Virginia* (Lanham, Md.: Rowman & Littlefield, 2000), 141.

56. Jon Butler, "Why Revolutionary America Wasn't a 'Christian Nation,'" in James Hutson, ed., *Religion and the New Republic: Faith in the Founding of America* (Lanham, Md.: Rowman & Littlefield, 2000), 198.

57. Library of Congress, "Faith of Our Fathers: Religion and the Founding of the American Republic," *LC Information*

Bulletin, May 1998, at http://www.loc.gov/loc/lcib/9805/rel igion.html; Thomas J. Curry, *The First Freedoms: Church and State in America to the Passage of the First Amendment* (New York: Oxford University Press, 1986), 194.

58. Ibid.

59. See Jon Butler's faculty home page, Religious Studies at Yale University, at http://www.yale.edu/religiousstudies/ cvjb.html.

60. "God and Country," *Flashpoints USA* with Bryant Gumbel and Gwen Ifill, at http://www.pbs.org/flashpointsusa/ 20040127/infocus/topic_01.

61. Ali Frick, "Butler breaks down Newdow 'under God' case," *The Yale Herald*, 9 April 2004, at http://www.yale herald.com/article.php?Article=3206.

62. "2004-2005 Courses in the History Department," Yale University History, at http://www.yale.edu/history/courselist ing.html.

63. John Demos, "Using Self, Using History . . .," *The Journal of American History* 89, no. 1 (June 2002): 37.

64. Roger Adelson, "Interview with John Demos—Social Historian of Early America," *Historian*, Spring 1993, at http://www.findarticles.com/p/articles/mi_m2082/is_n3_v55/ ai_13191877

65. Demos, "Using Self."

66. Anne D. Neal and Jerry L. Martin, "Restoring America's Legacy," A Report by the American Council of Trustees and Alumni, September 2002, 1.

67. David McCullough, "Why History?" National Book Awards Acceptance Speeches, The National Book Foundation, at http://www.nationalbook.org/nbaacceptspeech_dmccul lough.html.

68. S. Con. Res. 129, 106th Congress, 2nd session.

69. Charles J. Sykes, *The Hollow Men: Politics and Corruption in Higher Education* (Washington, D.C.: Regnery Gateway, 1990), 69.

Chapter 5

1. National Archives, "Declaration of Independence: The Signer's Gallery," *The National Archives Experience*, at http://www.archives.gov/national_archives_experience/char ters/declaration_signers-_gallery_facts.pdf, quoting American Council of Learned Societies, American National Biography (New York: Oxford University Press, 1999) and Who Was Who in America: Historical Volume 1607–1896 (Chicago: The A.N. Marquis Company, 1963).

2. National Archives, "America's Founding Fathers: Delegates to the Constitutional Convention," *The National Archives Experience*, at http://www.archives.gov/national_ archives_experience/charters/-constitution_founding_ fathers_overview.html.

3. Grutter v. Bollinger, 539 U.S. 332 (2003).

4. Duncan Kennedy, "First Year Law Teaching as Political Action," speech presented at the Second National Conference on Critical Legal Studies, 10 November 1978, *Law & Social Problems* 1, no. 47 (1980): 52.

5. Ibid., 47, 52, 53.

6. "Faculty Profiles—Robert A. Ferguson," Columbia Law School, at http://www.law.columbia.edu/law_school/communi cations-/reports/winter2003/r_ferguson.

7. Ibid.

8. Janet Halley, quoted in Elaine Ray, "'Don't ask, don't tell' a bad deal for gays in the military, Halley says," *Stanford Reporter*, 29 September 1999.

9. National Archives, "Constitution of the United States: A History," at http://www.archives.gov/national_archives_expe rience/charters/constitution_history.html, quoting Roger A. Bruns, A More Perfect Union: The Creation of the United States Constitution (Washington, D.C.: National Archives, 1986), 33.

10. Michael C. Dorf, "Create Your Own Constitutional Theory," *California Law Review* 87, May 1999, 593.

11. Richard H. Fallon Jr., "Stare Decisis and the Constitution: An Essay on Constitutional Methodology," New York University Law Review 76, May 2001, 596–97.

12. Morton Horwitz, "Is American Progressive Constitutionalism Dead?: II. Ethical and Historical Themes in Progressive Constitutionalism: In What Sense Was the Warren Court Progressive?" *Widener Law Symposium* 4, Spring 1999, 98.

13. Frank Michelman, "The Republican Civic Tradition: Law's Republic," *Yale Law Journal* 97, July 1988, 1496.

14. Cass R. Sunstein, "Justice Scalia's Democratic Formalism," *Yale Law Journal* 107, November 1997, 567.

15. Horwitz, 96.

16. Ibid., 97.

17. Ibid., 99.

18. Ibid., 97.

19. 397 U.S. 358, 384.

20. "Remarks at the Opening Session of the National Conference on the Judiciary in Williamsburg, Virginia," 11 March 1971, Public Papers of Richard Nixon, 1971, 422.

21. "Remarks at the Annual Meeting of the American Bar Association in Atlanta, Georgia," 1 August 1983, Public Papers of Ronald Reagan, 1983, 1111–12.

22. "Special Message to the Congress on the Marshall Plan," 19 December 1947, Public Papers of Harry S. Truman, 1947, 515.

23. "Statement by the President on the Observance of Law Day," 30 April 1958, Public Papers of Dwight D. Eisenhower, 1958, 362.

24. "Address before a Joint Session of the California State Legislature," 5 September 1975, Public Papers of Gerald R. Ford, 1975, 1343.

25. Jean Shaw, "University of Chicago Transgender Activists Demand 'Gender Neutral' Bathrooms,'" ChronWatch,

1 December 2003, at http://www.chronwatch.com/content/ contentDisplay.asp?aid=5166.

26. Mary Anne Case, "Are Plain Hamburgers Now Unconstitutional? The Equal Protection Component of Bush v Gore as a Chapter in the History of Ideas about Law," *University of Chicago Law Review* 70, Winter 2003, 57.

27. David A. Strauss, "Must Like Cases Be Treated Alike?" University of Chicago, Public Law Research Paper No. 24, May 2002.

28. Gustav Kosztolanyi, "C S A R D A S: Blind Justice Crime and police corruption in Hungary," *Central Europe Review* 1, no. 5 (29 July 1999).

29. Alan Dershowitz, "Read Closely: The Ten Commandments Reflect a Primitive Worldview," *Los Angeles Times*, 14 September 2003, M5.

30. Michelman, 1495.

31. Peggy Cooper Davis, "Changing Images of the State: Contested Images of Family Values: The Role of the State," *Harvard Law Review* 107, April 1994, 1348–49.

Chapter 6

1. National Survey of the *Role of Polls in Policymaking*, The Kaiser Family Foundation, June 2001.

2. Joel Belz, "Missing the Point," *World*, 28 August 2004, 4.

3. Terry Mattingly, "Journalism Strategies in a Hostile Marketplace," 2001, at http://tmatt.gospelcom.net/tmatt/free lance/strategies.html.

4. Interview with Naomi Harralson, 20 February 2004.

5. Wm. David Sloan, ed., *Makers of the Media Mind: Journalism Educators and Their Ideas* (Hillsdale, N.J.: Lawrence Erlbaum Associates, 1990), 9.

6. John Leo, quoted in Brent Cunningham, "Re-thinking Objectivity," *Columbia Journalism Review* 42, no. 2, July/August 2003, 30.

7. "The Face and Mind of the American Journalist," Poynter Online, at http://www.poynter.org/content/content_view.asp?id=28235.

8. "Finding 4: Journalists Are More Likely to Be College Graduates," *The American Journalist in the 21st Century*, at http://www.poynter.org/content/content_view.asp?id=28790.

9. Ibid.

10. Interview with Naomi Harralson, 20 February 2004.

11. Harry D. Marsh and David R. Davies, "The Media in Transition, 1945–1974," in William David Sloan, *The Media in America: A History*, 5th ed. (Northport, Ala.: Vision Press, 2002), 461.

12. Bill Kovach and Tom Rosenstiel, *Elements of Journalism: What Newspeople Should Know and the Public Should Expect* (New York, N.Y.: Crown Publishers, 2001), 11.

13. Interview with Naomi Harralson, 17 February 2004.

14. Joseph A. Mirando, "Embracing Objectivity Early On: Journalism Textbooks of the 1800s," *Journal of Mass Media Ethics* 16, no. 1 (2001): 31.

15. Robert Luce, *Writing for the Press: A Manual*, 5th ed. (Boston: Clipping Bureau Press, 1907), 170–71.

16. Jesse Haney, *Haney's Guide to Authorship*, quoted in Mirando, 25.

17. David T. Z. Mindich, *Just the Facts: How "Objectivity" Came to Define American Journalism* (New York: New York University Press, 1998), 5.

18. Ibid., 8.

19. Brent Cunningham, *Columbia Journalism Review*, July/August, 25–26.

20. Ibid., 26.

21. Ibid., 30.

22. Ibid., 31.

23. Ibid.

24. Bob Zelnick, quoted in Charles Geraci, *Editor & Publisher* 137, no. 8, August 2004, 28.

25. Marvin Olasky, *Telling the Truth: How to Revitalize Christian Journalism* (Wheaton, Ill.: Crossway Books, 1996), 25.

26. Ibid.

27. Doug Ireland, "Republicans Relaunch the Antigay Culture Wars," *The Nation*, 20 October 2003.

28. *The New Republic*, 12 April 2004.

29. "About Dissent Magazine," at http://www.dissent magazine.org.

30. Todd Gitlin, "Appointment with Destiny," *The Washington Monthly*, January/February 2003, 53.

31. JournalismJobs.com, "Interview with Roger Cohn," December 2001, at http://www.journalismjobs.com/roger_cohn.cfm.

32. Douglas Foster, quoted in Baylee Simon, "Doug Foster Has Done It All," *Northwestern Chronicle*, 26 February 2004.

33. Ibid.

34. Douglas Foster, "Are You in Anthropodenial?" *New York Times Book Review*, 8 April 2001, 30.

35. "Joel Rogers," University of Wisconsin Law School— Faculty and Staff Profiles, at http://www.law.wisc.edu/fac staff/biog.asp?ID=396.

36. Joel Rogers and Joshua Cohen, "New Democracy Forum," *Boston Review*, at http://bostonreview.net/BR21.6/forum.html.

Chapter 7

1. See Kelly Monroe, ed., *Finding God at Harvard: Spiritual Journeys of Thinking Christians* (Grand Rapids, Mich.: Zondervan Publishing House, 1996).

2. "The Harvard Charter of 1650," in Richard Hofstadter and Wilson Smith, eds., *American Higher Education: A Documentary History*, vol. 1 (Chicago, Ill.: University of Chicago Press, 1961), 10.

3. "The Mission of Harvard College," Harvard University, at http://www.harvard.edu/siteguide/faqs/faq110.html.

4. "Statutes of Harvard, ca. 1646," *Hofstadter and Wilson*, vol. 1, 8.

5. From a sermon entitled, "The Christian Preacher's Commission," delivered before the General Association of Connecticut, 22 June 1831 (New Haven, Conn.: Hezekiah Howe, 1831) (accessed from electronic version at http://www.mun.ca/rels/restmov/texts/dasc/tcpc.htm).

6. George Paul Schmidt, "Colleges in Ferment," *The American Historical Review* 59, no. 1, October 1953, 27.

7. True titles of current course offerings—see course catalog at http://www.harvard.edu.

8. Alexander Fraser Tytler, *Elements of General History, Ancient and Modern*, with a continuation by Edward Nares (Concord, N.H.: Isaac Hill, 1824), 281.

9. Louis Agassiz, *Essay on Clarification*, quoted in "Louis Agassiz (1807-1873)," University of California, Berkeley, Museum of Paleontology, at http://www.ucmp.berkeley.edu/history/agassiz.html.

10. First two titles by Mark Hopkins and Francis Bowen; modern titles by University of Chicago Law School professor Catharine MacKinnon and Yale-educated history professor George Chauncey, also at the University of Chicago, respectively.

11. Description of the class "Self-Fashioning: Dressing for Science and Medicine" by history professor Londa Schiebinger at Stanford University, at http://www.stanford.edu/dept/HPS/schiebinger.html.

12. Theodore Dwight Woolsey, "Sermons Preached Chiefly at Yale College" (New York: C. Scribner & Co., 1871), 399; "Duke to Permit Same-Sex Unions in University Chapel," *Duke Dialogue News Release*, 8 December 2000, at http://www.duke news.duke.edu/news/dialogue_newsrelease289b.html?p=all&id=2135&catid=46

13. George M. Marsden, *The Soul of the American University: From Protestant Establishment to Established Nonbelief* (New York: Oxford University Press, 1994), 99.

14. George P. Schmidt, "Intellectual Crosscurrents in American Colleges, 1825–1855," *The American Historical Review* 42, no. 1, October 1936, 47.

15. Frederick Rudolph, *The American College and University: A History* (Athens, Ga.: University of Georgia Press, 1990), 3.

16. Ibid., 6.

17. E.g., see Lawrence A. Cremin, *American Education: The National Experience 1783–1876* (New York: Harper & Row, 1980), 404–405, and Gladys Bryson, "The Emergence of the Social Sciences from Moral Philosophy," *International Journal of Ethics* 42, no. 3, April 1932, 308.

18. "An Account of the College of New Jersey in 1754," in Hofstadter and Smith, vol. 1, 93.

19. Rudolph, 17.

20. Ibid.

21. Marsden, 53; young Jonathan Edwards, then a student at Yale, wrote to his father after an uprising over food, "As soon as I Understood [Isaac Stiles, age 21] to be One of them, I told him that I thought he had done exceedingly Unadvisedly and told him also what I thought the Ill Consequences of it would be, and quickly made him sorry that he did not take my advice in the matter."

22. Ibid., 4.

23. Alexander Fraser Tytler, *Universal History: From the Creation of the World to the Beginning of the Eighteenth Century*, vol. 1 (Boston: Hilliard, Gray, and Company, 1837), 473.

24. Herbert Baxter Adams, *The Study of History in American Colleges and Universities* (Washington, D.C.: GPO, 1887), 54.

25. Ibid., 18.

26. William Smyth, *Lectures on Modern History: From the*

Irruption of the Northern Nations to the Close of the American Revolution, "new" ed., vol. 2 (London: H.G. Bohn, 1854), 473.

27. *A People's History,* 90; Smyth, vol. 2, 511–12.

28. Smyth, vol. 2, 514.

29. Louise L. Stevenson, *Scholarly Means to Evangelical Ends: The New Haven Scholars and the Transformation of Higher Learning in America, 1830–1890* (Baltimore, Md.: The Johns Hopkins University Press, 1986), 3.

30. Leonard Bacon, quoted in ibid.

31. Francis Bowen, *The Principles of Metaphysical and Ethical Science Applied to the Evidences of Religion* (Boston: Hickling, Swan, and Brown, 1855), 40–41.

32. *Washington Post,* 1 February 1993, 1. On the following day the *Post* made a correction: "There is no factual basis for that statement."

33. George M. Marsden, *The Soul of the American University: From Protestant Establishment to Established Nonbelief* (New York: Oxford University Press, 1994), 92; Ralph L. Ketcham, "Moral Philosophy," *The Journal of Higher Education* 24, no. 7, October 1953, 366.

34. Ketcham, 367.

35. Hofstadter and Smith, vol. 1, 275.

36. "Yale Laws of 1745," ibid., 54.

37. Ibid.

38. Gordon Wood, "Forum: The Creation of the American Republic, 1776–1787: A Symposium of Views and Reviews, Ideology and the Origins of Liberal America," *The William and Mary Quarterly* 44, no. 3, July 1987, 628–40.

39. James Hutson, *Religion and the Founding of the American Republic* (Washington, D.C.: Library of Congress, 1998), 31–32.

40. Ibid, 35.

41. Jeremiah Day, "The Christian Preacher's Commission," delivered 22 June 1831 (New Haven, Conn.: Hezekiah Howe, 1831), text available http://www.mun.ca/rels/restmov/texts/dasc/tcpc.htm.

42. Authors Mark Hopkins, William Paley, and Francis Bowen.

43. Francis Wayland, *The Elements of Moral Science* (Boston: Gould & Lincoln, 1856), 45, 47, 350.

44. Bryson, 306.

45. Ralph L. Ketcham, "Moral Philosophy," *The Journal of Higher Education* 24, no. 7, October 1953, 364.

46. Francis Lieber, "On History and Political Economy, as Necessary Branches of Superior Education in Free States," quoted in Daniel C. Gilman, ed., *The Miscellaneous Writings of Francis Lieber,* vol. 1 (Philadelphia: J.P. Lippincott & Co., 1881), 181, 183.

47. Ketcham, 364, 369.

48. Schmidt, "Colleges in Ferment," 20, 27.

49. Gladys Bryson, "The Emergence of the Social Sciences from Moral Philosophy," *International Journal of Ethics* 42, no. 3, April 1932.

50. William Whewell, *The Elements of Morality, Including Polity* (New York: Harper & brothers, 1856), 161.

51. Francis Wayland, *The Elements of Moral Science* (Boston: Gould & Lincoln, 1856), 341.

52. Stevenson, 64–65.

53. Ibid.

54. "Yale Laws of 1745," 54.

55. Schmidt, "Colleges in Ferment," 32.

56. Tytler, *Universal History*, 421.

57. Ibid., 422–23.

58. Francis Bowen, *The Principles of Political Economy Applied to the Condition, the Resources, and the Institutions of the American People* (Boston: Little, Brown, and Co., 1859), 21–24.

59. Ibid., 22–23.

60. Ibid., 23.

61. Smyth, 392.

62. Ibid., 408.

63. Wayland, *Elements of Moral Science*, 355.

64. Schmidt, "Intellectual Crosscurrents," 59.

65. Philip Lindsley, "Philip Lindsley on the Condition of the Colleges," quoted in Hofstadter and Wilson, 245.

66. Tytler, *Universal History*, 464-65.

67. Francis Lieber, "History and Political Science Necessary Studies in Free Countries," *The Miscellaneous Writings of Francis Lieber*, vol. 2 (Philadelphia: J.P. Lippincott & Co., 1881), 357.

68. See Lamar Alexander, "Putting the Teaching of American History and Civics Back Into Our Classrooms, Out of Many, One: E Pluribus Unum," Heritage Lecture No. 784, 14 March 2003, The Heritage Foundation, at http://www.her itage.org/research/education/hl784.cfm.

69. Joseph Story, *Commentaries on the Constitution of the United States: With a Preliminary Review of the Constitutional History of the Colonies and the States, before the Adoption of the Constitution*, vol. 2 (Boston: Little, Brown, and Co., 1858), 687.

70. Kenneth Umbreit, *Founding Fathers*, quoted in Meldrim Thomson Jr., "James Otis: Earliest Patriot of the Revolution," *One Hundred Famous Founders* (Orford, N.H.: Mt. Cube Farm, 1994), 371.

71. B.J. Lossing, "John Hancock," *Biographical Sketches of the Signers of the Declaration of American Independence* (New York: George F. Cooledge & Brother, 1848), 26.

72. David McCullough, *John Adams* (New York: Simon & Schuster, 2001), 18–19.

73. George Pellew, *John Jay*, American Statesmen Series, vol. IX (Boston: Houghton, Mifflin and Company, 1898), 320, vii.

74. Drew R. McCoy, *The Last of the Fathers: James Madison and the Republican Legacy* (New York: Cambridge University Press, 1989), 20, quoting Madison's friend and contemporary, Edward Coles.

75. K. Alan Snyder, *Defining Noah Webster: A Spiritual Biography* (Washington, D.C.: Allegiance Press, Inc., 2002), 252.

76. John T. Morse Jr., *John Quincy Adams*, American Statesmen Series, vol. XV (Boston: Houghton, Mifflin and Company, 1898), 304, vii.

77. Albert Bushnell Hart, *Salmon Portland Chase*, American Statesmen Series, vol. 28 (Boston: Houghton, Mifflin, and Company, 1899), 435.

78. Washington College was the first institution of higher education chartered in America after independence. Its founder and first president, the Reverend William Smith, was highly active in both educational and evangelistic ventures throughout his lifetime. Although Washington College claims that its founding was "secular," the writings of William Smith reveal that his emphasis was quite the contrary. For example, here is the text of the first prayer that Smith wrote to publish in a book for students: "O Almighty, and most merciful Father, my Guardian and Protector, both by Night and Day, I humbly thank Thee for adding one more Day to my Life. Grant, I beseech Thee, it may not, thro' any Fault of mine, be a Day of Reproof and Shame to me. Incline my Heart to adore and serve Thee, and to honour and obey my Parents and Instructors, and to love them for the Care they take of me. O my God, make my Improvement in Knowledge and Goodness answerable to the Opportunities Thou art graciously pleased to favour me with. Thy Blessing only can enable me to do this; and I most humbly and earnestly pray for it, in the Name and thro' the Mediation of my blessed Saviour and Redeemer. *Amen*" (Philadelphia: B. Franklin and D. Hall, 1753). See also the commencement address below.

79. M. E. Bradford, "George Mason," *Founding Fathers: Brief Lives of the Framers of the United States Constitution*, 2nd ed. (Lawrence, Kans.: University Press of Kansas, 1994), 149.

80. Lossing, "Richard Henry Lee," 167.

81. William Wirt, *Sketches of the Life and Character of Patrick Henry*, 15th ed. (New York: Derby & Jackson, 1857; reprint Purcellville, Va.: Home School Legal Defense Association, 1998), 31.

82. Ibid.

83. William Smith, *A Charge: Delivered May 17, 1757, at the first anniversary commencement in the college and academy of Philadelphia, to the young gentlemen who took their degrees on that occasion* (Philadelphia: B. Franklin and D. Hall, 1757), Schoenberg Center for Electronic Text and Image, University of Pennsylvania, available at http://dewey.library. upenn.edu/sceti/printedbooksNew/index.cfm?textID=cur tis_608&PagePosition=1.

Concluding Thoughts

1. Ravi Zacharias, *Can Man Live without God* (Nashville: Word Publishing, 1994), 36.

2. Ibid., 35.